TEENS

and the

DEATH PENALTY

Elaine Landau

—Issues in Focus—

ENSLOW PUBLISHERS, INC.

Bloy St. and Ramsey Ave.   P.O. Box 38
Box 777   Aldershot
Hillside, N.J. 07205   Hants GU12 6BP
U.S.A.   U.K.

Library of Congress Cataloging-In-Publication Data

Landau, Elaine.
    Teens and the death penalty / Elaine Landau

        p. cm.—(Issues in focus)

    Includes bibliographical references and index.

    Summary: Chronicles the history of the death penalty in America,
with an emphasis on its application to teenagers.

    ISBN 0-89490-297-0

    1. Capital punishment—United States—Juvenile literature.
2. Capital punishment—United States—History—Juvenile literature.
3. Juvenile corrections—United States—Juvenile literature.
4. Juvenile corrections—United States—History—Juvenile
literature. [1. Capital punishment—History.] I. Title.
II. Series: Issues in focus (Hillside, N.J.)

HV8699.U5L36   1992

364.6'6'0973—dc20   91-23351

                                  CIP

                                    AC

Printed in the United States of America

10 9 8 7 6 5 4 3 2 1

Cover photo: Wide World Photos

Contents

Preface

Many Americans have been affected, in one way or another, by the recent rising tide of violent crime. In searching for a solution to what has become a national dilemma, considerable differences of opinion have emerged. At one end of the spectrum, individuals advocate new social programs to curtail crime-breeding conditions; at the other, those favoring capital punishment view it as a valuable crime deterrent and believe the death penalty should be meted out to both adults and juveniles guilty of murder.

This book is about capital punishment, especially as it relates to young people. Through an examination of both historical data and present-day facts, it reveals how capital punishment evolved in America and the factors perpetuating it. My research has led me to believe that seemingly just punishments aren't always just and that it is inappropriate for the leading nation of the free world to kill young people, even if these minors have taken the lives of others. Read the arguments and evidence within these pages and decide for yourself.

Elaine Landau

1

The Establishment of Capital Punishment in the United States

Sixteen-year-old Harley Beard died on December 14, 1914. He hadn't suffered from a fatal illness, been the victim of a devastating automobile accident, or found himself trapped in a burning building. Instead, the teenager had been a death row inmate at an Ohio penitentiary, and on that cold December day it had been his turn to occupy the electric chair.

The boy, who had formerly worked as a farm hand, had been continually harassed and abused by his employer. Initially, Harley had attempted to adjust to the difficulties he'd experienced at work, but after a time he felt unable to endure the farmer's treatment of him any longer. Eventually, the boy's pent-up rage erupted into violence as he brutally struck back at the man who had taunted him. Unfortunately, Harley Beard killed his employer as well as the man's mother and sister.

Society's retribution came swiftly for young Beard. He was convicted of the murders and sentenced to die. With the boy's death, some felt that justice had been served. However, others were significantly less comfortable with Harley Beard's sentence. They wondered if the wayward teen, whose IQ bordered on mental retardation, had been completely responsible for his actions. Beard had cited "bad company, cigarettes, and intoxicating stimulants" as factors contributing to his behavior.

Yet, regardless of anyone's opinion on his sentence or the circumstances surrounding his case, Harley Beard's life was taken from him prior to his seventeenth birthday. The final stay of execution he had eagerly awaited never came. Harley's last words before the electric current was turned on were, "I think it is awful to send me to my Heavenly Father in this way." [1]

Capital punishment is not a new phenomenon. Its use dates back through the centuries. Death sentences had been pronounced and carried out prior to the existence of formalized courts. In early societies prior to 2000 B.C. a father even had the right to condemn another family member to death if he determined that a grievous wrong had been committed.

Developing civilizations frequently established codes of justice that incorporated capital punishment. Often these early measures may have seemed exceedingly harsh. For example, in ancient Greece, the leader and lawmaker Draco prescribed the death penalty for what are presently considered minor offenses. Someone found guilty of laziness or of stealing a piece of fruit would be executed as swiftly as a murderer might be.

Draco's political opponents argued that his laws were written in blood rather than ink. Yet the Greek lawmaker defended his reasoning, stating that those guilty of lesser crimes deserved to die. His only regret was that a greater penalty could not be extracted from the individuals who had committed heinous offenses against society. Even today the term "Draconian measures" is generally used to imply harsh action.

In 500 B.C., over a thousand years after Draco's laws had prevailed in Greece, the laws of Rome proved to be only slightly more lenient. There an individual could be sentenced to death for disturbing the peace late at night, starting a fire, or stealing crops. In fact, throughout Europe, a trend toward harsh laws and somewhat severe punishments continued to prevail as the years passed. During the Middle Ages, capital punishment, usually imposed through excessive torture or death by fire, was extremely widespread.

By the 1600s in England, over two hundred offenses were punishable by death. And when the British colonists arrived in the New World, they tended to model their laws after those of their homeland. In accordance with the English penal code, the new settlers invoked the death penalty for a number of crimes. Basically fourteen offenses were considered capital crimes, although there was some variation among the colonies as to how the laws were carried out.

During this period, offenses such as witchcraft and vagrancy were among those crimes punishable by death. Usually colonial death sentences were delivered within a religious context. In determining a person's guilt and sentence, those in charge often relied on the Bible to justify their actions, and they usually proved quite able in finding biblical quotations to condone the fate that eventually befell the condemned colonists.

In fact, the death penalty might await any person who broke one of the ten commandments, and at the time both adults and minors might be subjected to capital punishment. The first teenager known to be executed in colonial America was a sixteen-year-old boy named Thomas Graunger. He was hanged for having engaged in beastiality (a sexual act involving an animal). As deliberations in his case centered on biblical interpretations, the boy's fate seemed sealed from the start.

His accusers simply quoted the Bible passage that read, "And if a man lie with a beast, he shall surely be put to death, and ye shall slay the beast." Accordingly, the mare, cow, and all the young calves involved in the incidents with Graunger were killed as well.

In early America, the death penalty was not resorted to whimsically but instead became an integral part of the written codes by which the various colonies governed themselves. Some of these laws specifically addressed the fate of young people. For example, the 1650 common code of Connecticut stated that a boy sixteen years of age or older could be put to death for deliberately disobeying either his father or mother.

Although most of the colonies staunchly adhered to harsh judicial codes reminiscent of English law, there were some exceptions. For example, the Quakers, who served as a dominant force in southern New Jersey, forbade the use of capital punishment regardless of the crime. Similarly in Pennsylvania, the use of the death penalty was restricted to the crime of murder.

Generally, in areas where applicable, death sentences tended to be imposed on males. Yet as the years passed and the nation continued to grow, young females met their fate at the gallows as well. Among those executions recorded was that of a twelve-year-old African-American girl known only as Eliza. In 1868 Eliza had been employed by the Graves family of Kentucky as a servant. Among her other household duties, it was Eliza's responsibility to care for Walter, the couple's two-and-a-half-year-old son.

Early on in her employment, Eliza seemed to get on well enough with the small boy. Walter always enjoyed playing games with Eliza and following her around as she completed her various chores. No one had ever noticed any unpleasantness between the two. However, one evening shortly before supper, Mrs. Graves realized that Walter wasn't in the yard where he was supposed to have been playing. The little boy had last been seen going to the barn with Eliza and several other children, but he hadn't returned with the rest.

After an extensive search for the missing toddler, Walter was found in a nearby wooded area. It looked as if the small boy had been hit over the head with a large rock. The child died before the night was over.

Since young Walter had been under Eliza's care, she immediately became a suspect. Yet when initially questioned, the twelve-year-old firmly denied having any knowledge of the incident. Nevertheless, she had already become the object of the townspeople's rage, who felt certain Eliza was lying.

When her case came to court, a stream of witnesses was produced to testify against Eliza—although in a number of instances their objectivity was questionable. The prosecution's witnesses had even included the dead boy's parents. As had been anticipated, the jury quickly reached a guilty verdict. Eliza's request for a new trial was denied. Instead, the judge set the twelve-year-old's execution date.

On the scheduled day, several hundred men and women came to see Eliza's hanging. As the girl climbed the steps to her death, dressed in a plain black gown, she trembled with fear. It was expected that the execution would be over quickly, but as it turned out, the young girl didn't die easily. Instead, her body seemed to twist and jerk violently in midair. Then after several minutes, Eliza was still. The life of the preteen girl had finally been extinguished. Once her body was cut down, some spectators requested pieces of the hanging rope as souvenirs.

Although executions such as Eliza's had become fairly common, an examination of America's Constitution reveals scant reference to the death penalty. Unlike the codes that had governed the colonies, nowhere in the document does it state that capital punishment is required by law. In fact, the only segments of the Constitution that appear to assume the death penalty's existence are two amendments in the Bill of Rights.

These amendments offer additional protection to individuals charged with crimes for which the death penalty might be imposed. The Fifth Amendment makes specific mention of capital crimes, and both the Fifth and Fourteenth amendments prohibit the state from depriving an individual of life without due process of law.

Due process of law is the procedure by which persons accused of crimes are assured of fair treatment by the judicial system. It guarantees that an accused individual will be informed of the charges against him or her and will receive an unbiased trial. It also ensures that all criminal codes be written in a comprehendible manner so that everyone may be aware of what constitutes an illegal act. In addition, due process guarantees that a person's accuser will not sit in judgment of him. Due process embodies an important American ideal. Fairness under the law is especially crucial in capital cases as a person's life is at stake.

Yet even with the protections afforded by due process, some individuals still firmly believed that capital punishment was immoral. They grew determined to protest the growing number of state laws that sanctioned the death penalty as an acceptable form of punishment. Perhaps the person most frequently associated with the beginning of the movement to abolish capital punishment was Benjamin Rush.

Rush, one of the signers of the Declaration of Independence, spoke out openly against state-sanctioned executions. Stressing that the state lacked the inherent right to forfeit the lives of its citizenry, Rush sought other alternatives to deal with criminals. Among these were his plans to establish a house of reform or a type of prison in which individuals convicted of capital crimes would be detained while undergoing a rehabilitative process.

Rush spent years of his life writing and disseminating pamphlets on the evils of the death penalty. He continually refuted the most common biblical quotations given in defense of capital punishment. Rush even argued that the inherent violent nature of capital punishment would be more likely to increase rather than deter other violent acts.

Eventually, Rush won the support of a number of prestigious and politically influential Philadelphians. In fact, his efforts may be at least partly responsible for restoring a reform first passed in colonial times that outlawed capital punishment in Pennsylvania for any crime other than murder. Before long Michigan was also swayed by abolitionist sentiment and in 1846 repealed its statute for state execution. A trend seemed to be spreading as Rhode Island banned the death penalty in 1852 and Wisconsin did the same shortly thereafter.

Although death penalty abolitionists achieved success in some states, in other areas an entirely different sentiment prevailed. At times executions, which were frequently held publicly, became something of a curiosity. The somber mood often associated with the loss of a human life sometimes gave way to what was considered by some as a grotesque carnival-like atmosphere.

For example, a triple hanging of three young teenage boys on June 25, 1880, drew a crowd of over ten thousand people to the public square at Canton, Ohio, where the execution was to take place. In order to accommodate the large crowds wishing to witness the executions, railway companies added special excursion trains running from Pittsburgh and Chicago to the Ohio destination.

The actual hanging took place just before noon. Then the boys' bodies were cut down and placed within the jail's hallway. During the following four to five hours, crowds of people filed by the corpses in order to get a better look at the bodies.

With the passage of time, capital punishment largely continued throughout much of America. In some instances, cases challenging the death penalty were brought before the Supreme Court. However, frequently these had more to do with the technical means by which executions were performed than with the question of the death penalty's validity. For example, in 1890, the United States Supreme

Court upheld the use of the electric chair as an appropriate means of execution.

But in the years that followed, capital punishment abolitionists managed to challenge the constitutionality of the death penalty before the Supreme Court. In one such case, it was argued that capital punishment violated the Eighth Amendment, which prohibited cruel and unusual punishment. However, the Court refused to establish an unwavering definition of "cruel and unusual punishment." Instead, it ruled that a definition of cruel and unusual punishment must reflect "the evolving standards of decency that mark the progress of a maturing society." To the abolitionists' disappointment, numerous Gallup polls and other surveys in the early 1900s demonstrated that the American people overwhelmingly supported the death penalty. This prevalent attitude seemed to suggest that capital punishment did indeed reflect the society's overall standards of decency.

Nevertheless, the abolitionists continued their efforts. Although the Deep South was reluctant to alter its capital punishment statute, some of the Middle and North Atlantic states sharply reduced the number of offenses for which the death penalty could be imposed. Even in instances of homicide, state legislatures began to specify distinctions between first- and second-degree murder as well as expressly define premeditated murder. Before long, abolitionist organizations such as the American Society for the Abolition of Capital Punishment sprang up in areas where sentiment for their cause seemed strongest.

In some instances, states repealed their laws in response to specific incidents. That's what happened in Minnesota in 1906, when an English immigrant named William Williams was executed. On May 20, 1905, a jury had found Williams guilty of first-degree murder in the death of a teenage boy. Since at the time Minnesota law made the death penalty mandatory for such convictions, Williams was sentenced to die.

Williams's lawyer appealed his case to the Minnesota Supreme Court. In his client's defense, he argued that the jury had been prejudiced in their decision-making by highly sensationalized newspaper accounts of the crime. However, Williams's attorney was unable to convince the higher court. The jury verdict and accompanying sentence were upheld. The prisoner would hang after all.

At the appointed hour, Williams was brought to the scaffold, where he saw the tall gallows for the first time. As he stood ready to die, his last words were, "Gentlemen, you are witnessing an illegal hanging. I am accused of killing Johnny Keller. He is the best friend I ever had." [2]

At that point, Williams said good-bye to the priest who had counseled him in the weeks prior to his execution date. Then the sheriff's deputies tied Williams's arms and legs tightly with leather straps. A black hoodlike cap was pulled over the condemned man's head as his neck was thrust through the hanging noose. The only thing left for the sheriff to do was pull the lever to open the trap door beneath Williams.

However, unknown to the sheriff and his deputies, a number of crucial factors hadn't been taken into account, perhaps partly because there hadn't been a hanging in the county for over a decade. As a result, the sheriff and the men who worked along with him were somewhat inexperienced in the technical aspects of an execution.

Nevertheless, they'd tried their best to overcome their lack of expertise in these matters by checking twice the equipment they'd be working with. Only the day before, the sheriff had tested the rope with weights to be certain that the thick cord would not snap under the pressure of the prisoner's body.

Believing that everything was in perfect order, the sheriff pulled the lever to initiate the execution. Williams's body dropped through the trap door opening, but it was immediately apparent that something had gone wrong. The condemned man was still very much alive.

As it turned out, the rope used to hang Williams had been too long. With so much slack in the cord, the prisoner merely fell to the ground with his feet breaking the fall. His body never swung from the rope as intended. Apparently, the sheriff had failed to estimate accurately just how much the rope would stretch. The pull of Williams's weight on the rope had lengthened it by about eight inches. To worsen matters, the condemned man's neck had stretched nearly four and a half inches during the ordeal.

The sheriff and his deputies used the rope to hoist Williams back up again. They did not cut down the body, but instead allowed the condemned man to choke to death in midair. It took the prisoner nearly fifteen minutes to die.

When details of the hanging mishap were reported in the newspapers, the public became outraged. Even some proponents of the death penalty were put off by the cruel and barbaric nature of the hanging. In fact, when the sheriff submitted his reimbursement bill for the execution expenses, the County Board of Commissioners refused to honor his payment request.

Within weeks of Williams's execution, a movement arose to abolish capital punishment within the state. In March of 1906, the International Abolition Society (to prohibit the death penalty) was established with its international headquarters in Minneapolis. This organization endeavored to end capital punishment in such areas as Minnesota and California, as well as outside the country in England and South Africa.

The momentum that began with William Williams's execution continued to grow. Governor Johnson had originally signed Williams's death warrant, but less than a year later, in 1907, he'd been quoted as saying, "I believe that capital punishment is a relic of the days of barbarism. I am personally opposed to the legal sanction given hanging for the crime of murder." [3]

As a result of Williams's hanging, Minnesota State Representative George McKenzie introduced new legislation to ban capital punishment in the state. Finally one of his proposed bills passed both the state house and senate. Capital punishment was now outlawed in Minnesota. McKenzie's bill was passed just in time to save two convicted felons from the hangman's noose. As other states had taken similar initiatives, by 1917 twelve states had banned capital punishment within their borders.

But death penalty abolitionists soon learned that their victories were often short lived. Public sentiment for and against capital punishment seemed to waver with both economic and crime fluctuations. At times large numbers of people, convinced that the death penalty deters crime, expressed concern for their safety once this final punishment could no longer be extracted.

As legislators tended to respond politically to the immediate concerns of their constituents, many states abolished capital punishment only to reinstate it at a later date. This vascillation became characteristic of numerous states. For example, although Maine abolished the death penalty following the Civil War, the voters changed their minds shortly thereafter and demanded that it be put back on the law books. But within the next twenty years, public opinion shifted for a second time, and it was abolished once again.

Drafting capital punishment legislation is a complex task because in the United States the death penalty may be imposed for crimes against either the state or federal government. Generally, states have limited their use of capital punishment to murder offenses, although in some states it may also be imposed for specified crimes that result in the death of an individual—such as in armed robbery, kidnapping, or hijacking.

Thirty-four federal offenses are punishable by death. Among these are treason, espionage, the assassination of the president, kidnapping, taking a hostage, killing a foreign official, and murder for a fee. The death penalty may also be imposed on major drug dealers involved in narcotic conspiracies.

In order to create reasonable capital punishment legislation, other important questions must be dealt with within a larger context. Among these is the issue of executing juveniles. At times states permitting capital punishment have handled the question by having their state legislatures designate a specific age at which such punishment was deemed appropriate. In some instances, state legislatures have altered these age limits as public opinion dictated. In other states, no minimum age was set, and cases involving young people were evaluated on an individual basis.

Minimum Ages for Execution by State

STATE	AGE	STATE	AGE
Alabama	14	Montana	12
Arkansas	14	Nebraska	18
California	18	Nevada	16
Colorado	18	New Hampshire	17
Connecticut	18	New Jersey	18
Georgia	17	New Mexico	18
Idaho	14	North Carolina	17
Illinois	18	Ohio	18
Indiana	16	Oregon	18
Kentucky	16	Tennessee	18
Louisiana	15	Texas	17
Maryland	18	Utah	14
Mississippi	13	Virginia	15
Missouri	14		

States With No Minimum Age for Execution

Arizona	South Carolina
Delaware	South Dakota
Florida	Washington
Oklahoma	Wyoming
Pennsylvania	

Areas Without the Death Penalty

Alaska	New York
Hawaii	North Dakota
Iowa	Rhode Island
Kansas	Vermont
Maine	Washington, D.C.
Massachusetts	West Virginia
Michigan	Wisconsin
Minnesota	

Some have argued that death penalty age variations existing among states are inherently unfair. Other moral and legal problems have arisen as well. Although the Constitution guarantees individuals due process prior to the imposition of a death sentence, this hasn't always been the case. Depending on financial as well as other circumstances, at times death row inmates have not received adequate legal representation. For example, following one man's execution, it was learned that his attorney had only spent a total of eight hours in preparing the condemned man's defense. An attorney who had handled another executed inmate's case had been trying to juggle nearly three hundred other cases at the same time.

It was also frequently argued that capital punishment was unconstitutional as it wasn't uniformly administered throughout the nation. For example, in some states, a man who killed a victim during a robbery might be sentenced to life in prison. Yet in another state, an accomplice who didn't pull the trigger but stood alongside the murderer or perhaps drove the getaway car might be sentenced to death.

Since the death penalty was so often meted out in such a haphazard fashion, many wondered if justice was being served. As a result, a moratorium on the death penalty, backed by the Supreme Court's authority, was called from 1967 to 1976. The Court had not concluded that the death penalty itself was unconstitutional. It had merely ruled that under certain state statutes capital punishment had not been administered in a fair and uniform way. The Court determined that the manner in which the death penalty had been applied actually constituted "cruel and unusual punishment"—thereby violating the Eighth and Fourteenth amendments to the Constitution. Supreme Court Justice Potter Stewart cited that capital punishment had often been applied "freakishly" as if the accused person "had been struck by lightning."

As a result of the Supreme Court's decision, thirty-nine state capital punishment laws, as well as those of the District of Columbia, were struck down. Across the nation, over six hundred prisoners who had awaited their fate on death row would now have to return to court to be resentenced.

Attempting to contend with the Court's decision in the years that followed, thirty-six states drew up new capital punishment statutes. Through these laws they had to develop ways to ensure fair and uniform sentencing practices. Some states established "guided discretion" laws.

These statutes clarified procedures that the sentencer (either a judge or jury) was required to follow prior to imposing the death penalty on a defendant. Such laws tried to ensure that those doing the sentencing were fully knowledgeable as to which factors within a case were appropriate for consideration in determining a sentence.

The "guided discretion" laws adopted by numerous states were upheld by the Supreme Court. As these areas passed new capital punishment statutes, courts began to impose the death penalty with increasing frequency. Within the first six years following the Court's approval of the new state laws, only a handful of individuals were executed. However, the number of executions increased with the passage of time.

As executions became more common, they became less newsworthy. In some instances, where no prior notoriety surrounded an incident, often only a single reporter from the condemned person's hometown paper came to cover the event. As one Texas prosecutor said, "The executions are now back [in the newspapers] with the obituaries, which is where they belong. There's less tendency to glamorize the executed defendant and more of a feeling that he got what he deserved." [4]

Yet on some occasions, executions have evoked something of a carnival atmosphere reminiscent of the public hangings of the early 1800s. For example, when Velma Barfield, a North Carolina grandmother, was executed for poisoning her fiancé, a boisterous crowd assembled near the prison. They chanted over and over, "Kill her, kill her," and "Burn Bitch Burn." [5]

Perhaps circuslike festivities reached their peak in 1989 with the Florida electrocution of serial killer Ted Bundy. Vendors surrounding the prison sold plastic electric chair pins and tasteless bumper stickers bearing such slogans as "This Buzz Is for You" and "Roast in Peace." Some described the atmosphere as being much like a college football rally. In fact, over three hundred college students had gathered. Many carried banners with such slogans as "Thank God It's Friday." When the crowd was informed that Bundy had died, whistles and whoops filled the air. Some spectators even set off firecrackers.

Law enforcement officials weren't favorably impressed with the raucous display. As Assistant Chief James Sewell of the Florida State University campus police said of the public demonstration, "It makes a sham of the criminal justice process. We are carrying out a serious concerted effort to bring a hideous case to a close." [6] Perhaps one elected official best described the frequent general furor and fascination that surrounds some executions when he said, "The public has been mesmerized by the electric chair." [7]

It is difficult to deny the seemingly increased national appetite for the death penalty as more Americans appear to view this final punishment for both adults and juveniles as just retribution. Further legal attempts to overturn the death penalty on the grounds that it defies present societal "standards of decency" have been denied by the Supreme Court. Instead, the Court has held, "In part, capital punishment is an expression of society's moral outrage at particularly offensive conduct." [8]

2

Why People Favor or Oppose Capital Punishment

"The eyes of a psychopathic killer are a chilling sight. I have looked into the eyes of more than one cold blooded murderer— and wished them dead." [1] These are Alice Coddington's words—a woman presently doing volunteer work with the families of murder victims. Alice has personally experienced their feelings of loss. Within nearly a one-year period, her cousin as well as a very close friend were murdered. Both women had been killed while at home caring for their small children.

At one time, Alice Coddington had been against capital punishment. However, she no longer feels that way. As she said:

> Before these murders, I still had a trusting conviction that killers had temporarily gone astray and could be redeemed somehow—perhaps by society, perhaps by God. My conviction now is that God has nothing to do with murder. It is an individual's crime against society, and the proper punishment should also be meted out by society. [2]

There are a substantial number of individuals in favor of capital punishment. Many believe that someone who terminates the life of an innocent person deserves to forfeit his own life. Frequently, to justify their position, death penalty proponents cite the biblical quotation—"An eye for an eye." In many instances, advocates of capital punishment have stressed that families of homicide victims frequently receive worse treatment than their relatives' murderers. Often grieving family members are too easily forgotten in the judicial shuffle following a homicide. It's been argued that although the rights of the accused are carefully guarded, the victim's family has few if any rights whatsoever. Individuals who favor the death penalty stress that although capital punishment cannot bring back the dead, it at least assures the victim's family that the killer will not go on living while their loved one lies in a grave.

Capital punishment proponents further argue that the death penalty serves as a deterrent against future crime. They stress that a would-be murderer who is certain he'll be executed for his crime will be more likely to think twice before acting. When confronted with statistical evidence to the contrary, some capital punishment proponents have stressed the undeniable reality that the execution of a murderer at least stops that person from ever killing again. Generally, those in favor of the death penalty are also not moved from their viewpoint by the risk of executing an innocent individual. They argue that the truth will surely surface during the trial process.

Capital punishment advocates strongly feel that the death penalty should be used when appropriate in states where it's the law. They fear that juries and judges who avoid this type of sentencing may be inadvertently expressing a form of contempt for an important aspect of our legal system. They reason that if those responsible for enforcing state statutes deliberately avoid doing so, then it will be nearly impossible to expect criminals to respect and obey the law.

Many capital punishment proponents feel that juveniles who commit heinous crimes should be subject to the death penalty just as if they were adults. They believe that young people who engage in savage brutality have lost the innocence characteristic of youth and do not deserve preferential treatment.

It has been frequently argued that in instances in which juveniles commit horrific premeditated crimes, the death penalty may well be warranted. As Oklahoma Assistant Attorney General David Lee, who argued for a juvenile death penalty in front of the Supreme Court in 1981, stated, "If it's a horrible murder, and they're shown to be mature enough and responsible for their actions, then I don't see why they shouldn't receive the death sentence." [3]

Capital punishment proponents have frequently stressed that juveniles are only sentenced to death in rare instances, and in such cases they are often guilty of especially vicious crimes that entailed a significant degree of prior planning. As an attorney with the nonprofit Washington Legal Foundation, an organization that reviews court actions and protests lenient sentencing, explained, "Some kids are precocious killers and must be stopped. It's not necessarily a gross travesty of justice for a fifteen-year-old to receive the death penalty. I'd have few scruples about imposing it . . . because I don't think . . . age [always] operates as a mitigating circumstance." [4] To many individuals who hold this viewpoint, it doesn't matter whether a murderer is twelve or one hundred and two. They feel someone who has brutally stolen another's life must be held accountable for his actions.

Opponents of capital punishment see the situation differently. These individuals argue that over fifty scientific studies have clearly demonstrated that capital punishment does not serve as a crime deterrent. Among these is the research done by the National Academy of Science's Panel on Research on Deterrent and Incapacitative Effects. Ironically, the researchers found that in some instances

25

homicide rates actually fell slightly in a number of areas following the abolition of the death penalty.[5]

Use of the death penalty has sometimes been justified on the grounds that it is the only form of comparable retribution that may be offered to victims' families. Although some relatives and friends may wish to see their loved one's murderer die, this reaction is not true for everyone. As the parents of one young murder victim stated:

> We began to think about what Johnny would say if he could speak in court. We knew without question that he would have forgiven the person who shot him. . . . As the parents of a murder victim, we would like to see an end to the death penalty. We still long for our son, but we don't want anyone else's son or daughter killed in our name or in the name of justice.[6]

Perhaps among the most persuasive arguments against the death penalty is that each time the state takes a life, it does so in the name of the American people. Individuals who view the death penalty as cold-blooded institutional homicide do not want to be made unwitting accomplices to what they believe is a crime. They are against having their tax dollars used for this purpose.

Capital punishment opponents have also stressed that executing prisoners costs significantly more than maintaining them in prison. A recent estimate revealed that an average capital case in New York costs taxpayers three times more than supporting an inmate in prison for the duration of a life sentence.

The high price tag associated with death penalty incidence has to do with the exorbitant costs involved in providing legal representation and due process for death row inmates. These cases frequently entail numerous appeals. Therefore, the dollar and cents cost per case often skyrockets astronomically. For example, finding, investigating, and subpoenaing witnesses to court is a costly as well as a time-consuming endeavor.

At times, investigators needed to photograph and reconstruct crime scenes may command fees upwards of fifty dollars an hour.

Appropriations for the testimony of medical witnesses such as psychiatrists and pathologists can amount to more than a thousand dollars a day. As has frequently been the case in California, a capital offense trial can cost up to $4,000 a day and last one to two months.[7] Individuals against capital punishment feel that the process robs an already overburdened criminal justice system of what few resources are available.

However, this argument may soon lose some of its validity as the cost of death row appeals begins to drop. In May 1990, the Senate adopted an amendment that limits death row inmates to only one appeal in which to challenge the constitutionality of their sentence in federal courts. Previously, individuals sentenced to die had numerous opportunities to appeal their sentences. Nevertheless, capital punishment opponents believe that the reduced expense cannot justify the cost to one's humanity in taking human lives as retribution.

At times, people who want to see capital punishment ended have individually acted, hoping to make a difference. One such instance occurred in November 1986 when, just prior to leaving office, New Mexico's Governor Tony Anaya took a strong stand against the death penalty. Citing capital punishment as nothing short of "inhumane, immoral and anti-God," the governor reduced the sentences of the five inmates then on death row to life imprisonment. At a press conference before leaving office, Anaya had stated, "My personal beliefs do not allow me to permit the execution of an individual in the name of the state. For me to simply walk away now will make me as much an accomplice as others who would participate in their executions." [8]

Many opponents of the death penalty find state execution of juveniles particularly offensive. As stated in a recent report from the American Bar Association (ABA), "The spectacle of our society seeking legal vengeance through the execution of children should not be countenanced by the ABA." Advocates for juveniles on death row have also stressed that young offenders have frequently been shown

27

to be better candidates for rehabilitation than older inmates with extensive criminal records.

While there is some debate as to whether someone who is old enough to commit a murder is too young to die for the crime, death penalty opponents feel that at some point children must be considered too young to be held completely responsible for their actions. They stress that adolescence is frequently a tumultuous time for many young people—a period often characterized by inconsistent emotions and rageful outbursts.

A number of child development experts have indicated that many adolescents have not fully matured emotionally. Such a young person may intellectually know the difference between right and wrong but may lack an adult's impulse control necessary to curtail his actions.

Some also contend that preteens and adolescents are less able than adults to comprehend realistically the full ramifications and consequences of their actions. To underscore this point, an expert from the Child Study Center at Yale University had cautioned, "Just look at how unsuccessful we are at educating our young people about pregnancy and drug abuse."

Those strongly opposed to capital punishment for minors have suggested that individuals under eighteen years of age be exempt from the death penalty. Although eighteen may seen like a somewhat arbitrary dividing point, it is the age most frequently used to mark entry into adulthood for noncriminal purposes—such as eligibility to enter into a contract, serve on a jury, or vote. They feel that executing young people below this age is inhumane and may violate other state sanctions designed to protect minors. Such legal dualities have sometimes proved cruelly ironic. For example, at one time some states allowed fifteen-year-olds to be executed while other laws in the same states prohibited fifteen-year-olds from witnessing an execution. These statutes were designed to shield young people from a potentially traumatic experience.

Opponents of the death penalty for juveniles frequently stress the special horror they feel is inherent in executing young people. One such unnerving case might be that of a young African American named Willie Francis. When he was fifteen years old, Willie worked part time in a local drugstore in his hometown of St. Martinsville, Louisiana. His employer, Andrew Thomas, was a white pharmacist in his fifties. Thomas was a somewhat prominent figure in their small community. He owned the thriving pharmacy, was well respected by his neighbors, and happened to be the brother of the town's police chief.

Francis had initially done well at the pharmacy. However, one day an especially unpleasant incident occurred between the young man and his employer. It seems that Thomas was dissatisfied with some aspect of the boy's performance and had been particularly harsh in publicly admonishing Francis and insisting that he improve.

The confrontation left Willie with a strong desire for revenge, and unfortunately, on a night in November 1944, he decided to take action. Willie positioned himself behind some bushes near his employer's house, knowing that before long the pharmacy owner would be closing the store and returning home. When Andrew Thomas reached the door to his house, Willie sprung out from where he had hid and pointed a gun at his employer. Thomas tried to take the weapon away from the boy. As the two struggled for the gun, the weapon went off four times. Three of the four bullets hit Andrew Thomas. One bullet lodged itself in Thomas's chest, the remaining two entering the man's back. Terrified over what had occurred, Willie Francis reached for the wounded man's wallet and fled.

Andrew Thomas's body was discovered soon afterwards. However, no one was aware of the circumstances behind his death. The police investigation continued for nearly nine months. A reward of $500 was even offered for any information leading to the arrest and conviction of Andrew Thomas's murderer.

Shortly after Thomas's death, Willie Francis relocated to Port Arthur, Texas. But the public falling out that had transpired between Andrew Thomas and Willie Francis some months before led police to suspect that Francis might have been involved in his former employer's murder. Port Arthur authorities recognized Willie Francis from an interstate police bulletin and the teen was apprehended and returned to the St. Martinsville police for questioning.

By then, the available evidence began strongly to point to Willie Francis as the crime's perpetrator. For example, when the Texas police arrested Francis, they found the dead man's wallet on his person. Once in the custody of the Louisiana police, he fully confessed to what had taken place. A date was subsequently set for Francis's murder trial.

At first it was doubtful that the fifteen-year-old actually comprehended the degree of trouble he was in. As Willie Francis was unable to afford an attorney, he was forced to rely on the services of a public defender assigned him by the court. It might be easily argued that the accused youth received less than a suitable defense. His trial began on a Wednesday, and by the following afternoon he'd been convicted of first-degree murder. The day after that he was sentenced to die in the electric chair.

Prison officials initiated the necessary paperwork to have Louisiana's portable electric chair sent to the St. Martinsville jail for his execution. After legal appeals to higher courts had failed, there appeared to be nothing to stop the state from executing Willie Francis. Nothing, that is, short of a faulty electric chair.

On the day he was scheduled to die, Francis was escorted to the infamous "hot seat" by the prison warden and several guards. There he was thrust down into the seat as the various guards used the chair's leather straps to fasten the boy to the mechanism of his death. Before a black hood was placed over his head and neck, he softly said, "The Lord is with me."

Although Francis seemed prepared to die at that point, he survived. When the current was turned on, he'd only experienced a sensation that "tickled him a bit, but did not hurt much." Seconds later the teenager called out to the guards to remove the hood because it was hard for him to breathe with his head covered.

Shocked, the guards immediately rushed forward to take the cloth off Francis. Then for a moment they simply stood there amazed at what had transpired. Yet as it turned out, Willie Francis's survival was not the result of a miracle but instead had been due to a defect in the chair's wiring.

Willie Francis was escorted back to his death row cell while the electric chair was sent out for repairs. The incident was highly publicized, and although it soon became the object of many crude jokes, the condemned teenage boy had nevertheless been through a harrowing ordeal. His lawyers, who now felt their client had suffered inordinately, were granted a temporary reprieve so that they could present Willie Francis's plight before Louisiana's Supreme Court.

Francis's lawyers argued that subjecting their client to the trauma of execution again would constitute nothing less than cruel and unusual punishment, which is constitutionally prohibited. Willie Francis's attorney also based the teenager's court appeal on the assumption that Francis's initial mishap with the electric chair was actually "an act of God."

As a capital punishment case had never been previously appealed on this basis, the issue attracted a good deal of news media attention. However, Willie Francis's attorneys were unsuccessful in persuading the court. The justices ruled against Francis in a five to four vote.

Nevertheless, Willie Francis refused to give up. He'd already been put through the terror of a threatened electrocution. The teenager and his attorneys continued to fight for his right to live. For a third time, they petitioned the Board of Pardons for clemency. Yet, in the end, Louisiana authorities decided against showing mercy to Francis.

The boy spent his last days in his cell remembering what it felt like to be strapped into a death seat. The repaired electric chair was returned to the prison, and on September 29, 1944, Francis was made to relive the experience of being executed by the state. This time the teenager's body was carried from the execution chamber.

More recently, two cases involving juveniles on death row were also challenged in a higher court. Only in these instances the United States Supreme Court was to determine whether the execution of sixteen- and seventeen-year-olds was actually unconstitutional. Both proponents of capital punishment and those against it anxiously awaited this landmark ruling.

The cases being heard were that of *Kevin N. Stanford* v. *Kentucky* and *Heath A. Wilkins* v. *Missouri*. Stanford had been found guilty of first-degree murder in the shooting death of a twenty-six-year-old female gas station attendant in Jefferson County, Kentucky. He was seventeen at the time of the murder.

Stanford, along with his friend, had robbed a gas station at which the victim had been employed. The youth and his accomplice took about three hundred cartons of cigarettes, two gallons of fuel, and some cash from the register. Then they forced the female attendant into a car and drove out to a secluded area. There she was repeatedly raped and sodomized by both males. Before leaving, Stanford shot the girl both in the face and in the back of the head, killing her. A corrections officer who interrogated Stanford following the crime testified that the teenager's account of the incident had been as follows: "He said, 'I had to shoot her. She lived next door to me and she would have recognized me . . . . I guess we could have tied her up or something or beat [her up] . . . and tell her if she tells, we would kill her' . . . . Then after he said that, he started laughing." [9]

Following the seventeen-year-old's arrest, it was up to Kentucky's juvenile court to determine whether he'd be tried as an adult or a juvenile. In accordance with Kentucky law, a youth could be tried as an adult if he were charged with a capital crime or if he were over sixteen years of age and charged with a felony. Kevin N. Stanford's age and actions had satisfied both categories.

Kentucky's juvenile court held a hearing to determine how best to handle the case. The seriousness of the charges were considered, as well as the fact that on numerous past occasions the juvenile court had failed in its efforts to rehabilitate Stanford. It was therefore determined to be in the community's best interest for Stanford to be tried as an adult.

Kevin N. Stanford was found guilty of murder, first-degree sodomy, first-degree robbery, and receiving stolen property. He was sentenced to die. During the penalty phase of Stanford's hearing, witnesses related how the boy had spent his childhood in the homes of various relatives and had grown up without adequate family support and supervision. By the time he'd turned thirteen, he'd already developed a serious drug problem. After being in a number of juvenile treatment facilities, Stanford had been evaluated as lacking appropriate social interaction skills.

Stanford's case was appealed before the Kentucky Supreme Court, where his lawyers argued that their client should never have been tried as an adult because he was thereby denied his "constitutional right to treatment," which he would have automatically received had he been dealt with within the juvenile court system. But Kentucky's Supreme Court upheld the lower court's ruling. The higher court's research indicated that "there was no program or treatment appropriate for the appellant [Stanford] within the juvenile system." Kentucky's Supreme Court also concluded that such factors as Stanford's age and his possible rehabilitation had been taken into consideration by his trial jury in determining his culpability and sentence.

After Stanford's appeal was turned down by the Kentucky Supreme Court, Stanford's lawyers took his case to the United States

Supreme Court. There it was heard in conjunction with another case in which a juvenile had been sentenced to death—that of *Wilkins* v. *Missouri.*

When he was sixteen, Heath A. Wilkins had stabbed to death a twenty-six-year-old mother of two, who'd been working behind the counter of a convenience store he and an accomplice robbed. The court record reflects that Wilkins's goal had been to burglarize the establishment and kill "whoever was behind the counter" since "a dead person can't talk." [10]

Wilkins and his partner took liquor, cigarettes, some other merchandise, and about $450 from the cash register prior to murdering the witness. Then as his accomplice grabbed the woman to prevent her from escaping, Wilkins stabbed her. Wounded and bleeding profusely, she fell to the floor. As she lay there, Wilkins stabbed the victim three additional times—two of these wounds punctured her heart. Fearing for her life, the young mother begged her assailants for mercy, but instead Wilkins stabbed her four more times in the neck. Content that the witness would die momentarily, the teenager and his partner left the store.

As he was under seventeen years of age, Missouri law did not permit Wilkins to be tried as an adult unless the juvenile court's jurisdiction were first terminated. As in Stanford's case, it was up to the state's juvenile justice system to make this determination. In deciding if Wilkins should be tried as an adult, the juvenile court acknowledged that it had been unable to assist Wilkins in turning around his life when he'd been brought before the court for numerous other offenses. Other factors considered were the "viciousness, force, and violence" of the crime and the fact that Wilkins was only six months short of the minimum age at which he could be legally tried as an adult.

Once it was decided that Wilkins's juvenile status would be terminated, he was charged with first-degree murder, armed criminal action, and carrying a concealed weapon. The youth pleaded guilty to all charges.

Evidence given at his hearing revealed that Wilkins, like Stanford, had a troubled past. As a very young child, he'd endured extensive emotional and physical abuse. At times, his mother's beatings lasted as long as two hours. Ever since he'd been eight years old, Wilkins had been in and out of various juvenile correctional facilities. He'd been previously found guilty of burglary, theft, and setting fires. Perhaps Wilkins's violent side first became evident after he had killed several neighborhood animals for no reason and tried to poison his mother by filling her medicine capsules with insecticide.

Although the psychiatrists who examined Wilkins stated that he suffered from personality disorders, they nevertheless found him capable of distinguishing right from wrong. Wilkins was sentenced to die as Stanford had been. The court handed down the following judgment:

> The court finds beyond reasonable doubt that the following aggravated circumstances exist:
>
> 1. The murder in the first degree was committed while the defendant was engaged in the perpetration of the felony and robbery, and 2. The murder in the first degree involved depravity of mind and that as a result thereof, it was outrageously or wantonly vile, horrible or inhuman.[11]

In reviewing the case, the Supreme Court of Missouri upheld Wilkins's death sentence. Both Stanford's and Wilkins's cases were heard before the United States Supreme Court in the summer of 1989. The thrust of the attorney's argument in each case was that it was unconstitutional to sentence a juvenile to death as such an action violates the Eighth Amendment in that it constitutes "cruel and unusual punishment." Since in past instances, the Supreme Court had ruled that cruel and unusual punishment is that which is contrary to the "evolving standards of decency that mark the progress of a maturing

35

society," the defense attorneys hoped to prove that inflicting the death penalty on juveniles violated societal standards.

However, the defense failed in its efforts. In a five to four vote, the United States Supreme Court upheld the ruling of the lower courts in both cases. To explain the Court's decision, Supreme Court Justice Scalia indicated that of the thirty-six states allowing capital punishment, only twelve require offenders to have reached a minimum age of eighteen, while just three others maintain that the offender has to be at least seventeen years of age. He therefore concluded, "This does not establish the degree of national consensus this court has previously thought sufficient to label a particular punishment cruel and unusual." [12]

Perhaps the controversy surrounding capital punishment in America and its appropriateness for young people was best reflected in the divided opinions of the United States Supreme Court justices. Justice Sandra D. O'Connor, who agreed with the Court's decision, wrote:

> The day may come when there is such general legislative rejection of the execution of 16 or 17 year-old capital murderers that a clear national consensus can be said to have developed. Because I do not believe that day has yet arrived I concur . . . in its [the Court's] judgment. [13]

Yet the four dissenting judges felt otherwise. Supreme Court Justice Brennan expressed their sentiments, writing that ample evidence already exists to demonstrate that executing sixteen- and seventeen-year-olds constitutes cruel and unusual punishment. Stressing that the opinions of respected organizations can be considered indicators of contemporary standards of decency, Brennan stated that such groups as the American Bar Association, the National Council of Juvenile and Family Judges, and the National Commission on the Reform of the Federal Criminal Laws have argued that "state-sanctioned killing of minors is unjustified."

The judge added that a number of distinguished organizations had even filed legal briefs in support of the Court's striking down juvenile death sentences. These groups included the National Parents and Teachers Association, the National Council on Crime and Delinquency, and the Children's Defense Fund.

Justice Brennan also wrote:

> We have never insisted that a punishment [be] rejected unanimously by the States before we may judge it cruel and unusual. . . . This Court abandons its proven and proper role in our constitutional system when it hands back, to the very majorities the Framers [of the Constitution] distrusted, the power to define the precise scope of protection afforded by the Bill of Rights, rather than bringing its own judgment to bear.[14]

As might be expected, public reaction to the Supreme Court decision was varied as well. Many death penalty opponents felt that sanctioning the state's continued execution of juveniles was nothing short of methodical murder. There was also the feeling among some that the Supreme Court had betrayed the American people by the manner in which it had arrived at its decision. Perhaps Justice Brennan's words were best echoed by Richard Burr of the NAACP's Legal Defense and Educational Fund when he said, "If all the justices can do is survey the legislative scene and declare a winner, you don't need a court. All you need is someone who can count."[15]

Yet criticism of the Court's decision was tempered by the sentiments of a substantial number of Americans who believed the Court's ruling had been appropriate. Many of these individuals felt uncomfortable voiding juvenile death sentences as they feared it might reinforce the notion that someone can take the life of another without fearing for his own.

Applauding the Court's decision, Phil Caruso, president of New York City's Patrolmen's Benevolent Association stated:

These are sound decisions in keeping with what's happening on our streets today. We're talking about teenagers who have reached the age of intellectual maturity, who can distinguish right from wrong and who have committed heinous acts of premeditated deliberate murder. They should suffer the full consequences.[16]

In a nationwide poll conducted by *Time* magazine and CNN, the majority of those surveyed agreed with the Supreme Court decision on capital punishment.[17] So at least for now it looks as if youthful murderers will continue to pay for their crimes with their lives.

3

A Methodical Death

Some sixteen-year-olds have wonderful hopes for their future. They may be filled with energy and eagerly looking forward to securing a well-paying job or perhaps going off to college. Such young people may dream about how many children they'll have or the type of house or apartment they'll live in as adults.

However, the lives of teens on death row differ dramatically. Their dreams are frequently of a more immediate nature. Their aspirations often focus largely on the success of their impending appeal before a higher court. They can only hope that their lives will be spared. To many, a sentence of life imprisonment would be a welcome relief.

These young people cannot allow themselves to imagine what they might have become or where they might one day reside. Instead, much of their energy may be channeled toward not thinking about what it would be like to die in a fifteen-by-fifteen-foot execution chamber. As one teenage girl on death row, sentenced to die for a murder she committed when she was just fifteen years old, described it, "They act like as soon as they electrocute me, all the crime in the world will stop. . . . I can't dwell on it. That's what makes people on death row go crazy. You just have to go one day at a time and see what happens." [1]

In past eras, societies have employed a variety of methods to execute both adults and juveniles. At times, the convicted person's social status, as well as the nature of his crime, helped determine the way in which he would die. In Europe, executed noblemen were most frequently beheaded with a large swiftly swung sword. In such instances, it was essential that the executioner have a keen eye and powerful arms. Otherwise, the process could be slow, bloody, and exceedingly gruesome.

On the other hand, condemned common folk often did not even have an opportunity to fare that well. Depending on the time, area, and culture, individuals sentenced to die might be hanged, burned alive, or have their bodies broken on a wheel. There also did not appear to be a great deal of public sympathy for those condemned to endure these excruciatingly painful execution rituals.

Interestingly enough, death on the guillotine was seen as a humane advancement in the execution process. In the late 1700s, a French doctor, Joseph Ignace Guillotin, argued that using different execution methods for various classes of people was inherently unfair. To remedy the situation, he devised a swift flesh-slicing machine that he claimed would make executions quicker and less painful.

Initially, his invention was tested on various farm animals as well as on corpses from the public poorhouses. Before long, it was officially recognized by France as an improved execution method and in 1791 was used for the first time in the execution of a convicted forgerer. The device, which was named for its inventor, Dr. Guillotin, remained France's official execution method until the death penalty was banned there in 1981.

In the United States, prison inmates condemned to death have had to face execution by a variety of methods. These included hanging, electrocution, the gas chamber, and more recently lethal injection. Early on, perhaps the most common method was hanging.

In 1828, at fourteen, James Guild was hanged in Hopewell, New Jersey, for a crime he committed when he was just twelve. Guild was a clever young African American who had worked as a servant for a white man named Joshua Bunn. Guild was an able worker, who prior to his conviction for murder was thought to be somewhat shrewd if a bit mischievous.

However, the preteen's problems began on September 24, 1827, when his employer sent him to cut corn in a field bordering a neighbor's farm. The adjacent farm belonged to a white woman in her sixties. At one time the woman's son had borrowed a pistol from Guild's employer, and Mr. Bunn had asked Guild to retrieve the gun for him. As he was working so near to the neighbor's farmhouse, the twelve-year-old decided to take care of the task that day.

To his surprise, the neighbor, Mrs. Beak, was outraged by the request. Not only did she refuse to give Guild the gun, but she also screamed irrationally at him for having dared to ask for it. Furious over her treatment of him, James Guild struck the woman across the face.

Although he thought about leaving then, Guild feared that Mrs. Beak would report the assault to both his employer and the authorities. Hoping to avoid being discovered, he decided to finish what he'd begun. Guild hit the woman until she was unconscious. Thinking she was dead, he then quickly headed back to his employer's farm.

About three hours later, the woman's grandson arrived home to find her lying on the ground where Guild had left her. By then she'd lost a great deal of blood. Help was summoned, but it was too late. Mrs. Beak died later that evening.

The authorities questioned Guild about the woman's death, but he denied having seen her that day. However, local law enforcement officials continued to suspect him. On the following day, they brought Guild back to the dead woman's home, where he was vigorously questioned as to where he was at the time of her attack. As the frightened young person tried to vindicate himself during the interrogation, he ended up telling the police a number of contradicting stories. Eventually, the twelve-year-old broke down and tearfully stated the truth. James Guild was arrested and charged with the woman's murder. Soon afterwards, he was indicted for the crime and in May 1828 found himself on trial for his life.

In actuality, the only evidence the prosecution had against Guild was his confession. The judge ruled that Guild's initial confession was inadmissible in court as it appeared to have been coerced from him by the police. However, while awaiting his trial in his jail cell, Guild had confessed again. The prosecutor therefore relied on James Guild's second confession as the mainstay of his case.

At first, it was believed that Guild might be spared from the hangman's noose because of his age. At the time, New Jersey law specified that individuals under fourteen years of age lacked the mental ability to formulate a crime reflecting true criminal intent.

But the prosecutor, who wanted the death penalty for Guild, devised a unique courtroom strategy to override this state statute. He argued that despite James Guild's youth, he was "smarter than common Black boys his age." Attempting to balance the picture, the judge cautioned the jury to remember the defendant's youth as well as carefully to discern if Guild genuinely had the ability to commit a premeditated murder. The jurors were instructed to rule in Guild's favor if they had any doubts.

Guild's entire trial lasted barely two days. In addition, the jury deliberated for only about two hours before bringing in a guilty verdict. At that time, a guilty verdict for first-degree murder carried a mandatory death sentence. It seemed certain the young New Jersey farm hand would hang. Ironically, James Guild's superior intelligence had resulted in his undoing. Despite the judge's warning, the jury had obviously not carefully considered the emotional maturity of someone who had just turned twelve years old.

While confined in prison prior to his execution, jailers noted that although James Guild was intelligent, his behavior was often quite childlike. They seriously doubted whether he understood the full ramifications of receiving a guilty verdict for first-degree murder. For example, James collected a group of mice that had scattered across his cell and played with them as if they were toy soldiers. He even staged a play trial with a twelve mouse jury as well as a mouse defendant and rodent attorneys.

On his execution day, James Guild was escorted to the outskirts of town, where the gallows had been built for the occasion. When the executioner placed the noose around his neck and a black hood over his head, Guild immediately shook the hood off. As might be anticipated, he was less successful in ridding himself of the noose.

True to his reputation, James Guild remained quick thinking and resourceful even during the last moments of his life. When the gallow's trapdoor opened, Guild managed to stop his body from falling by clinging to the opening with his toes. Observers noted that even at this late hour, it looked as if the boy hadn't comprehended that the state was actually going to take his life. He still seemed to think it was all a game.

However, within seconds, the sheriff ended any illusions James might have had. He quickly climbed back up the gallows stairs and used his hands to pry the child's toes from the wood. From then on everything went as planned. The state had succeeded in executing its very young murderer.

As the years passed, new execution methods, which were supposedly both more efficient and humane, were introduced. Among these was the electric chair. Typically, this imposing solid oak structure has a high back as well as numerous attachments, which include heavy black-leather straps. The electric chair is placed in a small area known as the death chamber. On a wall behind the chair usually rests an open panel of coils and lights essential to its operation.

Once a condemned individual is placed in the chair, a team of law enforcement officers will immediately strap down his arms, legs, stomach, and chest. A cap is placed over the prisoner's head. The cap is made largely of a spongelike material enclosed in a leather casing. A piece of metal at the cap's top passes on the electric charge. The cap contains electrodes that are affixed to the condemned persons's scalp. There are also electrodes attached to the strap that binds the prisoner's exposed right leg.

The last piece of equipment affixed to the prisoner is the death mask. Most death masks are made of leather and consist of two parts. The top portion conceals the prisoner's forehead and eyes while the bottom section encases the cheeks and chin. Only the condemned person's nose remains uncovered.

Once the electric current is turned on, the prisoner's body may stiffen in a series of spasms. A slight trace of smoke may be seen near the chair's cap. When it is over, the body will go completely limp.

The process of electrocution is not benign. A substantial jolt of electricity transmitted via the attached wires passes through the condemned person's body. At times, large burns may result from the process. In some instances, smoke and even fire have issued from the wounds. A number of recorded cases report that up to three jolts of electricity were necessary to extinguish an inmate's life. During the intervals between currents, witnesses have seen some prisoners painfully gasping for breath. Sometimes even one of the straps holding the prisoner to the chair has burned off.

Prison officers do not touch the condemned person's body for at least three minutes following the execution. During this period, the body cools off. Immediately following the execution, the corpse is so hot that the fingers of anyone who touched it would blister. After an appropriate interval, a physician will check the body for a heartbeat. Once it has been ascertained that the prisoner has expired, the warden will announce that the court order has been fulfilled.

The time a condemned person actually spends in the electric chair is minimal in comparison to the overall process initiated by a death sentence. It begins with the prisoner's confinement on death row where he'll wait, hoping for a successful appeal of his case. Near the time of his execution, the prisoner may be moved to the death house. This structure is located near the death chamber, where the electrocution will take place.

During the twenty-four hours prior to the prisoner's execution, a process known as the death watch begins. The death watch team is composed of law enforcement officers from the prison. Each handles a small part of the death watch and execution procedure. The work involved in an execution is divided into precise segments to ensure that things go smoothly. This process is essential because if improperly done, an execution could last an inordinate amount of time. Other problems can occur as well. For example, if the generator has been set at too high a level, a major portion of the prisoner's body may be quite badly burned.

The death team's surveillance of the prisoner will continue until the execution. These officers try to meet the condemned person's needs during his last hours. They may offer the prisoner coffee and cigarettes as well as allow him to telephone relatives. By keeping the prisoner contented and calm, they hope he will not put up a struggle when the time comes to strap him in the chair. The condemned person may request just about whatever he wishes for his last meal. However, frequently those sentenced to die within hours do not demonstrate much of an appetite.

Prior to the electrocution, the prisoner will have his head, facial hair, and right leg shaved. The procedure is done in the presence of a number of prison officers. They stand around him in the event that the man becomes violent or tries to resist in some other way. As a further precaution, the prisoner's hands and feet remain cuffed.

Shaving the inmate helps the electrocution to proceed smoothly. The elimination of hair lessens resistance to the electric current. It also reduces the risk of skin burns. After the prisoner is shaved, he showers and puts on clothing fastened by Velcro instead of zippers and buttons in order to reduce body burns.

Death watch team members report that by the time most condemned individuals are led to the death chamber, they're already resigned to their fate. Usually they appear humble if somewhat limp as they are seated in the death chair. Yet no matter how detached from the situation the person appears, execution witnesses frequently claim that beneath the prisoner's visible passivity is a person painfully aware that his life is about to be taken from him.

In 1946, two fourteen-year-old African Americans, James Lewis, Jr., and Charles Trudell, were sentenced to die in the electric chair for a murder they'd committed in Natchez, Mississippi. Both teens had been employed by Harry McKey, a white businessman who ran a local sawmill. McKey was married and the father of seven children.

One night the two decided to rob McKey as he worked late at his office. They made off with nearly sixty-five dollars, but unfortunately they'd brought along a pistol, and McKey was shot while the robbery was in progress. Realizing that he had died, the teenagers moved the man's body to a nearby wooded area, where they hoped he'd remain undiscovered.

Over a week later, McKey's remains were found. At that point, Lewis and Trudell were questioned by the police. Both eventually confessed and were arrested. After their indictment for murder, it was decided that although the two were involved in the same crime, they'd have separate trials. Both trials resulted in the same verdict. Lewis and Trudell were found guilty and sentenced to die. The two young people's lawyers unsuccessfully appealed their cases before the

Supreme Court. They were also rebuffed in their pleas to the state's governor for clemency.

Meanwhile, the teenagers had captured the media's limelight. Many organizations and individuals across America felt they were too young to be put to death. Cards, letters, and visitors from other states urged Mississippi's governor to save the youngsters' lives. There was even a petition started by a young attorney named Thurgood Marshall, who later became the first African-American justice of the United States Supreme Court. Yet in the end, all their efforts proved fruitless. Although the executions had been delayed several times, eventually the day they were to die arrived.

During their time in prison, both inmates had continued to act very much like young teenagers. They'd read stacks of comic books and took turns playing the guitar. Their parents visited on Sunday afternoons, and two Catholic priests succeeded in reintroducing these young people to religion. Both James Lewis, Jr., and Charles Trudell spent the night before their execution in prayer with the priests. By morning they appeared calm and indicated that they were prepared to die.

However, one of their attorneys had a harder time resigning himself to the teenagers' fate. He felt there was a cruel irony in forfeiting the lives of children to demonstrate that killing is wrong. As the lawyer wrote in a local newspaper:

> It occurs to my mind that neither of the children is sufficiently large to fit into the various attachments of the electric chair. Therefore, I should like to respectfully suggest that we seat them as we do children at our dinner table, that we place books underneath them in order that their heads should be at the proper height to receive the death current; and I further urge that the books used for this purpose be the 'Age of Reason,' 'The Rise of Democracy in America,' a copy of the Constitution of the United States, and an appropriately bound edition of the Holy

Bible. Then, with one current of electricity, the state of Mississippi can destroy all simultaneously.[2]

As might be expected, the state chose to ignore the attorney's caustic recommendations. Instead, after the portable electric death instrument was transported to the Mississippi jail, adjustments were made so that a child-size occupant could be killed.

Another common execution method in the United States has been the gas chamber. The concept of gas-administered executions developed out of research performed during World War I. At that time, some scientists had conducted extensive research on the effects of various toxic chemicals on the human body. In 1924, the gas chamber was first used to execute a condemned prisoner in Nevada. Afterwards, the method was adopted by a number of states. It was thought to be a clean and efficient way to terminate a human life.

Typically, the gas chamber was housed in a small one-story building known as the death house. Within the small death chamber, there might be as many as two steel chairs since on some occasions double executions have been conducted. The inside of the death chamber may be surrounded by a number of glass panes. These windows allow witnesses to be present at the execution.

Prior to the execution, the condemned individual will be informed that he may wear whatever clothes he wishes to die in. However, he is warned that following his death, his garments will automatically become state property. These items will be put through a decontamination process and then destroyed.

Before the actual execution date, the death team of prison officers will go through a trial run. A pellet of the deadly sodium cyanide will be tested at a local hospital to ensure that it has retained its strength.

During the prisoner's execution, sodium cyanide will be dropped into a sulfuric acid solution to create cyanide acid gas. The gas fills the small chamber so that the inmate strapped in the death chair is forced to breathe it in. The prisoner will be bound firmly to the chair.

Both of his legs as well as his arms are securely held down by two sets of leather straps across each limb. The other straps hold down his chest and midsection. Even his head is strapped to the chair's metal headrest. The only parts of his body that he can move on his own are his fingers and eyes.

It has been argued that dying in the gas chamber is the only execution method that makes the condemned person an active participant in his own death. The reason is that it's impossible for the prisoner not to inhale the toxic substance that surrounds him. Before dying, the prisoner may experience severe muscle spasms or even convulsions. The time it takes for a prisoner to die in the gas chamber varies. If he takes deep, long breaths and doesn't fight his fate, he may lose consciousness in under a half a minute. However, if the prisoner panics and tries not to breathe or takes short, shallow breaths, he'll die in a very different manner. He may remain conscious for as long as fifteen minutes. While conscious, breathing will become excruciatingly painful for him. He may experience a severe choking sensation. Frequently, painful abdominal cramping results.

In one instance, an executed inmate had arranged to communicate what he experienced in the gas chamber with a reporter who was to witness his death. The men had worked out a series of finger signals to convey feelings. Just prior to slipping into unconsciousness, the dying man indicated that he was in agony.

Often gas chamber witness areas tend to be small and unadorned. Some have floors that slope down toward a drain in the middle of the room in the event that one of the witnesses becomes sick to his or her stomach. Some prisons have an ambulance waiting outside in case a witness becomes exceedingly ill or emotionally upset.

Once the prisoner has been pronounced dead, an exhaust fan at the top of the chamber is turned on. Usually the gas is dispersed through a roof vent. Prison officers wait about fifteen minutes before entering the death chamber to remove the corpse. Before walking in, they'll put on gas masks and rubber suits. Then they'll hose down the prisoner's body and chair with a garden hose.

The prisoner's clothing is removed, sprayed with a decontaminator, and later burned. The inmate's body is scrubbed with soap and water and placed in a body bag. The deceased inmate's family may claim his body for burial. If unclaimed, some prisons bury the bodies of executed prisoners in a cemetery where the institution may own a number of plots. In such instances, no funeral service is provided. No headstone will be placed at the grave. The person buried in the plot remains forever nameless.

Frank Loveless was executed in a Nevada gas chamber on September 29, 1944, for a crime he committed when he was fifteen. Even as a young boy, Frank had already been in trouble with the law a number of times. After having committed several robberies, young Loveless was placed in an Indiana reformatory. However, Frank Loveless and another young inmate escaped from the institution and headed west in a stolen car.

After arriving in Elko, Nevada, the pair decided to go their separate ways. The other boy kept the car they'd driven out in while Loveless stole a second car in Elko. The owner reported the car stolen, and when a police officer spotted the vehicle on the highway, he pulled Loveless over to the side of the road. The fifty-six-year-old officer who stopped Frank Loveless was A. H. Berning—a grandfather who'd been an active member of the police force for over twenty-six years.

Although Loveless had pulled his car over, he resisted arrest. In a struggle between the two over the officer's service revolver, Berning was shot twice. Although the first shot only grazed the police officer, the second proved to be more deadly. Loveless ran from the highway, leaving the seriously wounded police officer to die in the stolen car parked at the side of the road.

Within a short time, officers in a second patrol car found the dead policeman. Frank Loveless was picked up shortly thereafter.

Following a lengthy interrogation, Loveless confessed to Berning's murder the next day. Perhaps finally coming to grips with what he'd done, the young person then spent most of his time crying in jail while awaiting trial.

Meanwhile, local residents had become incensed over the brutal slaying of a popular and well-respected local law enforcement officer. Berning's wife, two daughters, and four grandchildren were consoled at his funeral by a huge throng of mourners. However, the local newspaper, sensing that the residents might cry for blood, ran the following editorial:

> There should be some means of bringing this youth to trial so that he may be incarcerated in the Nevada state prison. The supreme penalty can hardly be expected, but he should be jailed for the rest of his life. . . . The people of this state will wish to see justice done in this case and will have no sympathy for a youth, regardless of the fact that he is only fifteen, who killed an officer of the law in such cold blood.[3]

Nevertheless, the teenager was tried, found guilty, and sentenced to death. While awaiting his execution, the boy converted to Catholicism. He regretted what he'd done as well as the price he'd now have to pay for his actions. Prison officials reported that Loveless cried the entire day before his execution.

On the morning of his death, the boy wrote letters to each member of his immediate family. All of Loveless's family still resided in Indiana, where he'd been born. As his last request, the teenager asked prison officials to "send some roses to my grandmother." Frank Loveless's death marked the first time anyone so young had ever been executed in Nevada.

In recent years, lethal injection has been heralded as the most benign form of execution. Some states offer condemned individuals a choice of the electric chair or lethal injection. When the idea of lethal injection as a means of execution was initially conceived, it was thought that executions could be modernized by having a doctor inject the condemned person with poison. Hopefully, capital punishment could be turned into just another aspect of medical science.

However, many physicians disagreed with this concept. The medical profession was quick to remind various correctional facilities of the Hippocratic oath, which states, "Neither will I administer a poison to anyone when asked to do so nor will I suggest such a course." As one physician who served as medical director at a department of corrections put it, "Murdering someone is not a medical procedure. I was trained in medical school to protect the health and welfare of humans. I was not trained to be a butcher." [4]

Once correction departments realized that doctors wanted no part of this procedure, the overall policy was altered. It was decided that although two physicians would be present at the execution site to verify that the prisoner was dead, the actual process would be performed by medically trained technicians.

When an execution through lethal injection takes place, the condemned individual is strapped to a hospital gurney in the death chamber. IVs are attached to him, and slowly a neutral saline solution begins to drip into the inmate's body. The machine that releases the actual poison is a compact boxlike instrument equipped with various dials and switches. In some instances, a button is pushed to release the poison into the saline solution. In other models, a plunger may have to be pulled to accomplish the deed. The drugs used to terminate the individual's life are often pancuronium bromide and potassium chloride. Both substances affect the heart.

Proponents of lethal injection as a method of execution claim that it allows the prisoner to die quickly. There are no burns or seizures as a result of the procedure—just the sound of a dying person clearing his throat for the last time.

Jay Kelly Pinkerton was executed by lethal injection in Texas on May 15, 1986. In 1979, Pinkerton, a seventeen-year-old, lived with his family in Amarillo, Texas. Although he worked, the teenager had found time to acquire an extensive police record.

The Laurence family, a young couple and their three children, lived in the same neighborhood as the Pinkertons. Mrs. Laurence was generally thought to be an especially attractive young woman. One evening while her husband worked the late shift, Jay Kelly Pinkerton broke into the Laurence residence, where he raped and killed Mrs. Laurence.

Before he finished with her, the teen had used a knife to mutilate the woman's body bizarrely. Then he left the home, taking the knife with which he had killed the wife and mother, as well as her purse. All the while the couple's three children had remained upstairs in their beds asleep.

When Mr. Laurence returned home later that night and discovered his wife's body, the police were called. Officers combed the area for suspects and acted on the few clues they'd been able to glean from the crime site. A witness had seen a young man fitting Jay Kelly Pinkerton's description leaving the Laurence home earlier that night. In addition, footprints from the Laurence house led police directly to the street where the Pinkertons resided.

The police went to Jay Kelly Pinkerton's home, but the boy's parents refused to let them in. When questioned as to the whereabouts of their son, both firmly stated that Jay had been home with them the entire evening. So although the case remained open, the police investigation appeared to be at a standstill.

Then several months later, a twenty-five-year-old former beauty queen was raped and murdered at the store where she worked. The woman had been stabbed to death and her body mutilated in much the same way Mrs. Laurence had been. The police assumed that the same person killed both women. At the time they were still unaware that Jay Kelly Pinkerton had struck again.

However, nearly a year after the Laurence murder, there was a break in the case. Checking their fingerprint files, a hand print left at the Laurence crime scene was identified as Pinkerton's. The teenager was arrested and charged with murder. Despite the defense's objections, a blown-up photograph of the victim's bloody and mutilated body was displayed for the jury throughout the proceedings. Pinkerton was found to be guilty as charged. After only an hour's deliberation, he was sentenced to die.

A lengthy appeals process followed the verdict. Then on August 15, 1985, when it seemed that all avenues for redress had been exhausted, Pinkerton was strapped to the prison hospital's gurney, where IVs were inserted into his arms. He lay there awaiting the lethal dose of poison that would end his life. But just then the phone rang. Pinkerton had been granted a stay of execution. The IV tubing was removed from his arms, and he was taken from the gurney back to his death row cell, where he awaited further word.

However, in time his stay was lifted, and Jay was assigned a new execution date of November 26, 1985. Then within ten hours of the time he was scheduled to die, still another stay of execution was granted. Pinkerton's third execution date was later set for May 15, 1986. The courts refused to grant him any more time, and he'd already exhausted just about every imaginable form of appeal. Pinkerton's mother personally delivered a petition to a federal judge pleading for her son's life, but her efforts could not save him.

As Pinkerton was strapped to the death gurney for the last time, he told the witnesses present to be brave for him. His father was permitted in the death chamber with his son. The last words ever uttered by Jay Kelly Pinkerton were to his father. The teenager just said, "Dad, I love you." [5]

4

The Irreversible Error: Executing an Innocent Person

When examining capital punishment, it is important to consider the inherent risk of executing the wrong individual. Although this might seem like an unlikely possibility, such errors actually do occur. A study by Hugo Bedau and Michael Radelet surveying eighty years of capital punishment in the United States determined that a significant number of these judicial injustices can actually be documented.

Their research revealed that during this time span, 139 innocent people had been sentenced to death. However, not all these individuals were executed due to such factors as reduced verdicts and sentences or new evidence coming to light resulting in exoneration. A total of twenty-three innocent persons are presently known to have been executed.

The researchers found that the most common reasons for these potentially horrific judicial mishaps included deliberately falsified testimony from witnesses for the prosecution, as well as general negligence on the part of both law enforcement personnel and individuals associated with the judicial process. Also contributing to the problem were unintentional errors by witnesses and others involved with the case.[1]

One unsettling instance in which an innocent person was wrongfully condemned to die occurred in 1975 in the case of an African American named Jerry Banks. While out hunting one afternoon in a wooded area near his Georgia home, Banks had accidentally stumbled on the corpses of two men. Startled by the discovery, he returned to the main road, where he flagged down the first passing car. Banks asked the vehicle's driver to report the bodies to the police, which the driver agreed to do.

Although shaken at first, Jerry Banks continued hunting and tried not to think about the grisly sight he'd witnessed. But as it turned out, it wasn't going to be easy for him to forget that day. Nearly a month later, Banks was arrested and charged with the murder of the two men he'd found in the woods. It might have seemed as if Banks had nothing to fear. He'd been at a neighbor's home at the precise time the coroner estimated the two had expired, and his neighbor willingly testified to that fact in court. Nevertheless, Jerry Banks was found guilty and sentenced to die.

Unfortunately, Banks hadn't been dealt a fair hand by local law enforcement officials from the start. Although the driver whom Banks stopped on the road had offered to testify, he was never called to do so. The man could have described Banks's initial reaction to the crime and told how Banks had urged him to report it to the authorities. Despite the fact that the gentleman had left his name and address so he could be reached easily, the sheriff and other law enforcement officials purposely withheld this information from Banks and his attorney. After this intentional suppression became evident, the Georgia Supreme Court granted Jerry Banks a new trial.

But Banks fared no better in his second trial. Once again, he was convicted of murder and sentenced to die. Some thought his poorly prepared court-appointed attorney might have been at least partly to blame for the verdict. Fortunately, following his second conviction, Banks was able to secure new legal representation. These attorneys ferreted out witnesses whose testimony proved to be extremely beneficial to their client's defense. The lawyers also made the court aware of the fact that Jerry Banks's hunting rifle couldn't have possibly been the gun that killed the two men.[2]

The newly uncovered evidence earned Banks the right to a third trial at which he was finally found innocent. All charges against him were dropped, and Jerry Banks was freed. Yet deliberate suppression of evidence and poor legal representation nearly cost him his life. Banks can also never be repaid for the seven years he spent in prison on death row wondering when his life would be terminated by the state.

While Jerry Banks was spared, not everyone else has been as fortunate. James Adams was an African American who received the death sentence after being convicted by an all white jury in March 1974 for the murder of a Florida white man. During his trial, as well as at his execution in May 1984, Adams had insisted that he was innocent.

Although he was identified as being in the vicinity of the murder, a witness who had seen the murderer leave the victim's home stated that the man had a considerably darker complexion than Adams and a mustache. Despite pleas from Adams's attorney, the Florida Department of Law Enforcement initially refused to provide the defense with a complete report of the evidence gathered. This refusal is particularly relevant since a hair found clutched in the victim's hand was shown not to be Adams's. Although this and other pertinent information surfaced after the trial, Florida's governor refused to grant Adams a stay of execution. Subsequent investigation into the case revealed that another man may have committed the crime for which Adams was electrocuted.

On March 15, 1988, Willie Jasper Darden, another African American, was executed in Florida for the murder of a white man. Like Adams, throughout the judicial proceedings, he swore that he was innocent. Following his conviction, two witnesses came forward providing additional evidence in Darden's favor. Unfortunately, as his case was not reopened, their testimony was never heard by a jury.

Although many law enforcement professionals are honest, hard-working individuals who actively seek justice, they are often subjected to intense public pressure to "solve the crime" or "find the killer." Often the news media may be impatient and critical of them when results or "headlines" aren't immediately forthcoming. Unfortunately, at times some police officers, prosecutors, and others within the criminal justice system have given in to the temptation to suppress evidence in order to close a case.

Other factors can act against a criminal defendant as well. Presently the entire court system is overburdened by an exceedingly large caseload. Proper case handling is crucial to the effective functioning of our legal system in all instances, but in capital cases it may literally become a matter of life and death. As stated in a report by the American Bar Association, "As currently funded, the criminal justice system cannot provide the quality of justice the public legitimately expects and the people working within the system wish to deliver." [3]

Perhaps one of the better known cases of an innocent person sentenced to die is that of Randall Dale Adams. Adams's ordeal began on Thanksgiving weekend in 1976. While hitchhiking on the highway, twenty-seven-year-old Adams had the misfortune to be picked up by sixteen-year-old David Harris. Although Adams didn't know it, Harris already had an extensive criminal record and had picked Adams up in a stolen vehicle. After riding together for a time, Adams asked to be dropped off at a motel where he planned to spend the night.

Although Adams had no knowledge of it, early the next morning while still at the wheel of the stolen car, David Harris gunned down Dallas police officer Robert Wood. When the killing was traced to the sixteen-year-old, Harris claimed he was innocent and blamed the murder on the hitchhiker he'd previously picked up—Randall Dale Adams.

The community was outraged by the vicious murder, and Dallas police were anxious to secure a murder conviction and execution date. Since at the time Harris was sixteen and seventeen was the minimum age for capital punishment in Texas, law enforcement officers chose to believe Harris's story and set their sights on Adams.

Although he had no previous record, the district attorney managed to convict and secure a death sentence for Randall Dale Adams. Not until several years later, in 1980, was his sentence reduced to life in prison so that prosecutors could avoid a retrial ordered by a higher court. Adams might have remained a convicted man had it not been for Errol Morris, a New York filmmaker, whose award-winning documentary film, *The Thin Blue Line,* had probed for new evidence that eventually helped Adams to win his freedom.

In Morris's film, witnesses to Officer Wood's murder cast serious doubt as to whether Adams could possibly have been the killer. During a new hearing for Adams, it became apparent that his initial trial had been largely characterized by deceptive testimony and withheld relevant evidence.

Meanwhile, as Adams waited in prison, the actual murderer, David Harris, had both turned seventeen and committed another murder. Once on death row after his conviction for the second murder, Harris confessed that he'd also killed the Dallas police officer. He claimed that he'd lied about Adams being the murderer because the former assistant D.A. who prosecuted Adams had promised him a deal if his testimony helped to convict the innocent man.

Finally, in March 1988, a Texas appeals court upheld a lower court's recommendation that Adams's conviction be overturned. As Judge M. P. Duncan stated, "[The] state was guilty of suppressing evidence favorable to the accused, deceiving the trial court . . . and knowingly using perjured testimony." [4] After twelve years in prison, Adams, whose only crime had been hitchhiking, was released.

Capital punishment opponents frequently cite the inherent danger of executing the wrong person. They stress that our judicial system is operated by human beings and that even under the best of circumstances no one's decision making is infallible. In Adams's case an innocent man was largely convicted on the testimony of a teenager, but some argue that at other times the circumstances could easily be reversed. In such instances an innocent young person, who hasn't really begun to live his life, might be deprived of doing so by the state.

Many of those in favor of capital punishment believe that the occasional execution of an innocent person may be the price we have to pay to maintain law and order in our society. Yet others strongly disagree, stressing that we cannot afford to sacrifice even one innocent life. They remind us that someday it could be our life or the life of a loved one.

5

Should a Nine-Year-Old
Be Executed?

James Terry Roach was executed in South Carolina on January 10, 1986, for a murder he committed when he was seventeen. Born the son of a truck driver in North Carolina, Roach had a childhood marked by troublesome incidents. Although he was sent to reform school as a teenager, he managed to escape when he was seventeen. At that point, Roach took to the road with a sixteen-year-old friend and a twenty-two-year-old former military police officer. The older man had both a shady past and a ready supply of alcohol and drugs.

In October 1977, while high on drugs, the three had been out driving along some back roads. When they came across a parked car, they pulled up to it to see who its passengers were. Inside they found a man, woman, and a fourteen-year-old girl. Almost immediately, Roach fired his gun three times into the man's head. With the male driver dead, the three dragged the teenage girl from the car. They raped the girl and then killed her as well. What happened to the woman was not reported.

When the trio was later arrested for the horrendous crime, their case was highly publicized. The public outcry was intense because many who heard of the incident clamored for the death penalty. Unfortunately, only one attorney was appointed to represent the three involved.

Since each defendant had manufactured a different and conflicting account of how the events had taken place, it became extremely difficult for any of them to receive unbiased legal counsel. The two teenage boys were also advised by the attorney to waive their right to a jury trial. The lawyer made this recommendation despite the fact that he had been warned that the judge was likely to deal harshly with the youths.

At his nonjury trial, Terry Roach pleaded guilty to murder and criminal sexual assault. Although the fact that he was a minor was taken into consideration by the court, Roach was nevertheless sentenced to death. In Roach's appeal of his sentence, attention was called to the fact that the teenager's extremely low IQ indicated that he bordered on being mentally retarded. A neurological study of Roach performed by physicians also revealed that at the time of the murders Roach may have also been in the early stages of Huntington's disease. This genetic brain disorder has been known to alter perceptions of reality as well as to play havoc with good judgment.

Although Roach's execution date was postponed four times, in the end his sentence was not commuted to life imprisonment despite the fact that numerous prominent individuals had spoken out on Roach's behalf. Among those who appealed to South Carolina's governor for clemency were Mother Teresa, Jimmy Carter, and UN Secretary General Javier Perez de Cuellar. But the governor declined to save Terry Roach.

The elected official was not unsupported in his decision. There were many people who strongly felt that Roach deserved to die. They believed that even someone with a child's IQ was somewhat responsible for his actions. As the prosecutor in Roach's trial said, "The boy . . . knows right from wrong. He is the meanest person I have ever met." [1] At the time, South Carolina Governor Richard W. Riley echoed his sentiments. Explaining his refusal to grant Roach clemency, the governor stated " . . . if we're going to have capital punishment, [Roach] . . . ought to be put to death." [2]

Once Roach resigned himself to his fate, he'd said of the death chamber, "Won't nobody have to drag me in there." The teenager proved true to his word. When his time came, he walked calmly to the electric chair at the Central Correctional Institution in Columbia, South Carolina.

After being strapped tightly into the device, Roach read from a statement that his lawyer held up for him. The young man had spent his last night alive writing the statement with the help of his mother and girlfriend. Although he had repeatedly practiced what he'd planned to say, he experienced difficulty pronouncing some of the larger words. Now as he sat in the electric chair about to die, Roach still stumbled on some words—not out of nervousness but because he was barely able to read. He basically said, "To the families of the victims, my heart is still with you in your sorrow. May you forgive me just as I know the Lord has done . . . . I pray that my fate will someday save another kid from the wrong side of the tracks." When he finished, the chair's lever was pulled, and Roach's body absorbed between 1,500 and 2,300 volts of electricity. He died about nine minutes later. As the scheduled hour of Terry Roach's death neared, a crowd gathered outside the prison compound. They had come to cheer the execution of an individual with a mental age of twelve for a crime he'd committed when he was seventeen.

It's been estimated that between 1976 and the late 1980s at least six of the ninety plus people executed in America suffered from some degree of mental retardation.[3] Mental retardation is a condition that impairs an individual's ability to learn as well as to adapt to social and behavioral norms. To be classified as mentally retarded, a person must have an IQ of 70 or below.

There are also different levels of mental retardation. According to the American Association on Mental Retardation individuals with IQs between 50-55 and 70 have "mild" retardation, while those whose IQs range from 35-40 to 50-55 are "moderately" retarded. An IQ of 20-25 to 35 indicates "severe" retardation, and "profoundly" retarded individuals have IQs of below 20-25. Nearly 90 percent of all mentally retarded individuals are classified as mildly retarded.[4]

Over the years, mentally retarded individuals have experienced significant difficulties within our criminal justice system. Although these individuals aren't any more prone to crime than the next person, an unusually large number of them end up in prison or on death row. In fact, the Clearinghouse on Georgia Prisons and Jails, a nonprofit Atlanta-based organization, estimates that approximately 250 mentally retarded inmates are on death rows throughout America.

This estimate may be at least partly the result of the fact that in countless instances these individuals have been read rights they don't understand and represented by attorneys who lack experience in handling the unique obstacles mentally retarded people face. The problem is further compounded when judges later find that they don't know what to do with the mentally retarded defendants appearing before them. As was cited in a report by the National Institute of Corrections, a division of the U.S. Justice Department, "Many mentally retarded inmates appear to be doubly damned. It is unlikely that they will receive special programming in corrections and even less likely that they will be transferred to other agencies where such special programming is more readily available."

Courts generally tend to treat mental retardation as if it were mental illness—although the two conditions are distinctly different. While mental illness may affect a person's ability to behave rationally, it can sometimes be treated with proper medication and therapy. But there's no "cure" for mental retardation. The condition, often caused by an injury to the brain, genetic factors, or inadequate prenatal care, is irreversible. Although a mentally retarded person may be capable of some learning, even with intensive individual tutoring, that person will remain retarded.

The American Bar Association has proposed developing more appropriate guidelines to deal properly with mentally retarded defendants within the criminal justice system. But at the present the situation remains problematic. Unfortunately, most states rule a person competent to stand trial if he is found to be "sane" by a court appointed psychiatric team. When tested in this manner, the majority of mentally retarded defendants will not be judged "insane." But in their case, the crucial question is not that of insanity, but rather whether or not they are fully able to understand the consequences of their deeds.

According to Miles Santamour, formerly on the President's Committee on Mental Retardation:

> All states have tests designed to determine competence from a mental-health aspect. But I don't think there is one state that has a good test to determine competency for a mentally retarded person.

Santamour added:

> Yet mental retardation can greatly interfere with the ability to make sound judgments, resist negative influences and even understand the nature or consequences of one's actions .... The majority of mentally retarded persons don't understand why it's wrong to steal, but they will say it's wrong to steal.[5]

Since there aren't adequate testing procedures to determine whether or not a mentally retarded person is fit to stand trial, many retarded individuals have been forced to endure court procedures they don't fully comprehend. The situation is worsened if the jury isn't completely aware of the extent of a mentally retarded defendant's handicap. To factually inform them of how mental retardation affected his client's thinking and actions, an attorney would need to call in costly expert witnesses. But as many mentally retarded defendants are unable to afford legal representation, they've relied on a court-appointed lawyer to defend them. If the judge in such cases determines that the state will not pay for these expert witnesses, the attorney will not be able to bring them into court. Therefore, the jury may remain only marginally informed about a condition that might have a significant bearing on their decision making and on the defendant's life.

Unfortunately, at times some mentally retarded defendants have hindered their own cases. While anxious to please authority figures in charge, they've actually confessed to crimes they never committed. Law professor James W. Ellis and his wife, special education professor Ruth Luckasson, are considered national authorities on the issue of mental retardation and criminal defendants. They believe that many mentally retarded inmates are innocent. As Luckasson explained:

> These people would do anything to cover up the fact that they are mentally retarded. That means boasting about crimes they may not have committed or acquiescing quickly to police officers in order to win their approval. ... What's more, mentally retarded defendants are often implicated by more sophisticated accomplices who end up with lighter sentences.[6]

That's what happened in the case of Jerome Bowden, a thirty-three-year-old retarded African American executed in Georgia's electric chair on June 24, 1986. Bowden had been convicted of the robbery and murder of a white woman in Columbia, Georgia. All the evidence against Bowden was gathered from Jamie Graves. Graves had been involved in the crime with Bowden but was offered a life sentence in return for his testimony against his retarded friend and cohort. Bowden's only other tie to the crime was the confession he'd made to the police following his arrest. His confession was accepted as valid despite a psychiatric evaluation of Bowden that revealed that "his actions stemmed primarily from mimicking those around him and from a strong desire to please, particularly those in authority." [7]

With an IQ of fifty-nine, Bowden had been long classified as mentally retarded. As a child, he'd attended five racially segregated schools, where he'd been placed in special classes for children unable to keep up with the others. Bowden, who had never been able to learn to read and write, was illiterate at the time of his trial.

Although Jerome Bowden's attorney tried to bring the issue of his client's competency into the trial, the presiding judge suggested that it be withdrawn. As a result, Jerome Bowden was sentenced to death by a jury who knew nothing of his diminished mental capacity.

The question of culpability and diminished mental capacity is not a new issue. Our nation's founders had attempted to deal with the matter early on. At the time the Bill of Rights was adopted, common law forbad the punishment of "idiots." During that period, this now derogatory term was used to refer to individuals so totally lacking in understanding that they would be considered severely or profoundly retarded by present-day standards. To their misfortune, mildly and moderately retarded persons generally continued to be executed without regard for their handicap. In some instances, these individuals were both mentally retarded and juveniles.

Such as the case of Hannah Ocuish—a twelve-and-a-half-year-old mentally retarded girl who had endured a brutal childhood. Hannah had never met her father, and her mother had been an alcoholic.

Hannah, along with her two brothers, was abandoned by their mother when they were still small. Initially, the children tried their best to survive on their own. They'd lie, steal, beg—do whatever was necessary to get through another day. The state had made several attempts to have Hannah live with a family, but these placements were unsuccessful. It was difficult for the retarded girl to follow directions carefully or complete the chores required of her to the satisfaction of the families with whom she lived.

Then in July of 1786, a terrible incident occurred that changed Hannah's life forever. One day Hannah spotted six-year-old Eunice Bollis walking down the street. Hannah had been cross with the young girl, who happened to be the daughter of a wealthy and influential Connecticut couple. It seems that several weeks before, Hannah had taken Eunice's basket of strawberries, and the child had run complaining to her mother. Mrs. Bollis saw to it that Hannah was punished, and Hannah had still not forgiven Eunice for telling on her.

That morning Hannah convinced the young girl to follow her to a deserted part of town. Then she knocked Eunice down and strangled her. Hannah tried to hide the body. However, the small girl's corpse was discovered the next day. When police questioned Hannah about the murder, she quickly made up a story about having seen four tall boys in the neighborhood whom she hadn't recognized. But when shown the young girl's bruised body, Hannah broke down and confessed to what had actually transpired. Confronted by what she'd done, Hannah was unable to stop crying. Moments later the police arrested her and escorted Hannah to a cell, where she remained until her trial.

Despite her initial confession, Hannah Ocuish's attorney advised her to plead not guilty. Hannah didn't seem terribly upset at her trial, but some believe that might have been due to the fact that the retarded girl hadn't actually comprehended that she could receive the death penalty. However, others in the courtroom appeared visibly moved as the brutal details of the case were revealed. At numerous times during the trial, the Judge seemed at a loss for words, and at least one of the jurors was seen drying his eyes.

Hannah was found guilty of murder. In determining her sentence, the judge took the girl's young age and low intelligence level into consideration. But these factors were not sufficient to save Hannah Ocuish's life.

On October 12, 1786, as she stood before him for sentencing, the judge said, "You have killed, and that in a barbarous and cruel manner, an innocent, helpless, and harmless child." Then he sentenced her to "be hanged with a rope by the neck, between the Heaven and earth, until you are dead, dead, dead." [8]

There was about a ten-week interval between the day twelve-year-old Hannah was sentenced and her execution date. At first Hannah seemed unusually calm. It soon became apparent to those surrounding her that Hannah truly wasn't aware of her trial's outcome. She hadn't understood that the judge had condemned her to death. It wasn't until someone explained her fate to her in words she was able to understand that Hannah became visually upset. The girl spent her last days in tears.

After climbing the scaffold on the day of her execution, Hannah looked about as if searching for someone to rescue her. But it was too late. The clergyman at the girl's side said a few words about the gravity of a sentence that terminates the life of a young person "who had never learned to live." Minutes later, Hannah Ocuish was dead.

Through the years the state's right to execute mentally retarded individuals has been challenged on a local and state level. However, in June 1989, the question was finally brought before the United States Supreme Court in the case of *Penry* v. *Lynaugh*.

Thirty-three-year-old John Paul Penry had been found guilty of rape and murder. The crime took place in October 1979, while Penry, who was employed as a delivery man, brought a refrigerator to the home of Pamela Moseley Carpenter.

When Penry arrived at her home, Ms. Carpenter had been using a pair of scissors to fashion Halloween decorations. Penry raped the woman and then stabbed her to death with her own scissors. But Pamela Moseley Carpenter did not die immediately. During the last hours of her life, she provided police with an accurate description of John Paul Penry. Penry was later picked up by the police and, following his arrest, confessed to the crime.

Testing revealed that Penry's IQ was somewhere between fifty and sixty-three. Psychologists determined that his mental age was equivalent to about that of a seven-year-old child. Penry's social and emotional maturity was similar to that of a nine-year-old's. Prior to his trial, Johnny Paul Penry was given a competency hearing. At that point, the court became aware of his limited mental capacity. Penry, who was unable to read and write, hadn't even completed first grade. A good part of his childhood had been spent in state institutions. But he was nevertheless found competent to stand trial.

While on trial, three different psychiatrists testified regarding Penry's sanity. The three physicians differed in their opinions, although all were in agreement that Penry suffered from serious mental limitations as well as from an inability to learn from past mistakes. Yet despite the facts presented and the physicians' testimony, Penry was convicted of capital murder and sentenced to death.

In subsequent appeals to higher courts, scant attention appeared to be given to the fact that Penry was illiterate, emotionally disturbed, and mentally retarded. A number of organizations spoke out in favor of repealing Penry's death sentence. As law professor James W. Ellis, who is also president of the American Association on Mental Retardation, argued:

> Of all the convicted murderers in this country, fewer than two percent are sentenced to death, and only a fraction of those are actually ever executed. The Supreme Court has held that the only constitutional basis for selecting those who can be executed . . . is the level of their personal responsibility for their crime. No

person with mental retardation is in that top one or two percent in his level of understanding, and foresight and responsibility.[9]

John Paul Penry lost his appeal. When the Supreme Court ruled that sixteen- and seventeen-year-olds could be executed, it also determined that mentally retarded individuals could not be categorically exempt from the death penalty. As Supreme Court Justice Sandra D. O'Connor wrote, "While a national consensus against the execution of mentally retarded people may someday emerge . . . there is insufficient evidence of such a consensus today."

She added:

Mentally retarded persons are individuals whose abilities and behavioral deficits can vary greatly. . . . reliance on mental age to measure the capabilities of a retarded person for purposes of the Eighth Amendment could have a disempowering effect if applied in other areas of the law. Thus, on that premise, a mildly retarded person could be denied the opportunity to enter into contracts or to marry by virtue of the fact that he had a 'mental age' of a young child.[10]

Although capital punishment opponents were disheartened by the decision, once again others felt the Court ruled wisely. Some had envisioned every murderer attempting to convince the jury of his retardation if mentally retarded individuals were exempt from the death penalty. And while numerous criminal justice professionals regard mental retardation as a serious impediment to a charged person's defense, not everyone feels that way. As one Texas prosecutor stated:

Some people regard mental retardation as a reason to totally excuse the crime that was committed. That's a position that I as a prosecutor cannot accept. If [a defendant] . . . is found competent, has a rational understanding of the proceedings, and is found legally sane, then certainly he is eligible for the death penalty.[11]

Since the 1989 Supreme Court decision, several mentally retarded inmates have been executed. More are scheduled to die. Though it might seem as if justice is finally being served, the sentiments expressed by Terry Roach's appeal lawyer following his client's electrocution have a haunting quality. He had said, "It was like executing a child." [12]

6

Race, Poverty, and Capital Punishment— the Deadly Connection

It has been argued that throughout much of America's history, racism has been an inherent factor in the application of the death penalty. African Americans, as well as other minorities, are discriminated against on a number of levels. Although African Americans comprise less than 13 percent of the population, approximately 42 percent of the inmates awaiting execution on death row are African American. Another 8 percent are members of various other minority groups.[1] Studies have revealed that an individual convicted of killing a white person is significantly more likely to receive the death penalty than those who kill African Americans. In fact, ninety-five percent of the victims of condemned prisoners are white.[2]

Instances of racism have also been cited in capital punishment cases involving juvenile offenders. No white female under the age of eighteen has ever been executed by the state. The only exception was a young Native American girl. Approximately 69 percent of the juveniles executed throughout America's history have been African

73

American, while 89 percent of their victims were white. Forty-three juveniles have been executed in the United States for the crime of rape. In each of these cases, the rape victims were white, while in every instance but one, the perpetrators were African American.[3]

James Arcene, a full-blooded Cherokee, was hanged for a crime he committed as a ten-year-old boy. At the time of the crime, the boy had been residing in Indian Territory in Oklahoma. One day he happened to be in a store with William Parchmeal, an adult male whom Arcene had known since he was a small child. The two looked on as an elderly Swedish man purchased a small item.

The Swede's name was Henry Fiegel, and after he exited the store, Parchmeal and the boy followed him as he walked toward a heavily wooded area. Parchmeal and Arcene snuck up on the unsuspecting man from behind and hit him over the head with a rock. Then William Parchmeal handed the ten-year-old a gun and ordered him to shoot the victim repeatedly.

Arcene fired four shots, killing the Swede. Then they left with several articles of Fiegel's clothing, as well as his money. Ironically, on the day he was robbed and killed, Henry Fiegel had only twenty-five cents left in his pocket.

Before long, people began to notice swarms of buzzards circling the area where Fiegel's body had been abandoned. The corpse was located and identified. Although Parchmeal and Arcene had been seen in the area and were initially suspected, charges were never pressed against them due to insufficient evidence.

But in the years that followed, a new deputy marshall became interested in the case. He revisited the crime scene, questioned witnesses, and eventually gathered enough evidence to issue an arrest warrant for Parchmeal and Arcene. Eventually the two stood trial for the murder they'd committed nearly twelve years before. However, as the jury was unable to agree on a verdict, their trial resulted in a hung jury. The prosecutor called for a new trial, and a year later both men found themselves in a courtroom again on trial for their lives.

Each man's attorney attempted to shift the blame for the incident onto the other defendant. But this strategy proved unsuccessful, and within two days the jury convicted both men. Parchmeal and Arcene were sentenced to hang for the crime.

The men had been tried in a special territorial court from which no appeals were permitted. As no other alternatives were available to them, both petitioned the president of the United States to intervene. But before long, they learned that no help would be forthcoming from that source.

Once Parchmeal realized that he would be executed, he confessed to his relationship with Arcene, revealing the ten-year-old's true role in the crime. Parchmeal admitted that he'd handed the child the gun and ordered him to shoot Fiegel. He noted that because the boy had been so young, he couldn't have possibly understood what he was doing.

Yet despite Parchmeal's confession, both men were hanged on June 26, 1885, at Fort Smith. Although at the time of his death, James Arcene was an adult, he was put to death for a crime he committed when he was only ten years old. Arcene's case is distinctive because he was the only person in America ever to be executed for a crime committed at such a young age. It's been argued that racism was a factor in the harsh sentence he received. Some feel Arcene would have been shown more mercy if he hadn't been a Native American.

Unfortunately, racism, which sometimes leads to the death penalty, may be an inherent aspect of the judicial process. Many minority group defendants are poor and unable to hire highly priced lawyers who have ample time and an adequate research staff with which to build a firm defense of their client. Therefore, as in many cases involving mentally retarded individuals, poor minority group clients are often represented by overburdened public defenders or court-appointed attorneys who frequently carry an inordinant number of cases and sometimes lack genuine enthusiasm for the task at hand. Sadly, in many instances, whether or not a defendant receives the death penalty is largely dependent on the quality of his legal representation.

Even in biblical times, it was widely recognized that wealth could influence the outcome of legal proceedings. In fact, the Old Testament specified that "the rich should have no advantage and the poor no disadvantage." Ideally, the principle of equal justice regardless of a person's economic or social standing within his or her community had been established. Yet this is often not the case for poor people who are frequently members of minority groups.

Competent legal representation is especially crucial during the sentencing phase of capital cases. The prosecution will argue that the death penalty is the only appropriate punishment for the individual on trial. However, in numerous instances, the Supreme Court has emphasized that at this point the defendant is given the opportunity to offer the court an account of any outside circumstances that might have influenced his behavior at the time of the crime.

The reasons presented would not serve to lessen the defendant's guilt but might instead show that to some degree he was not completely responsible for his actions. The defense attorney must show how these mitigating factors affected his client and prove that the special circumstances involved warrant a sentence of life imprisonment as opposed to the death penalty.

Often such mitigating evidence is readily available to a defense attorney willing to put in the time and energy to seek it out. It might be a matter of bringing in various experts to testify that the defendant has a personality disorder or that he's suffered from serious emotional problems.

At times relatives have been brought into court to tell how the defendant endured torturous years of abuse within a brutal home environment. In cases in which the defendant is a former soldier who has served in combat, veterans who served with him may be brought in to testify to the defendant's bravery under fire. They might also comment on how the cumulative effect of being on the front lines had taken its toll on the individual charged with the capital offense.

Although such mitigating factors can make the difference between the defendant spending his life in prison or being executed, in numerous cases, inefficient defense counselors have made little or no effort to seek out witnesses who could have saved their clients' lives. And in an overwhelming majority of these cases, these defendants have been minority group members.

As a Supreme Court clerk, who had observed the outcome of many capital punishment cases, stated, ". . . it is just as important to know that imposition of the death penalty frequently results from nothing more than poverty and poor lawyering." [4] These sentiments were reiterated by the American Bar Association, which has no official position on the death penalty. Yet the attorneys at an association conference agreed that 50 percent of all convicted death row inmates could have their sentences reduced if they were afforded adequate and competent legal representation.[5]

Armed with overwhelming statistical evidence that the death penalty is often tinged by racial bias, attorneys argued a case before the Supreme Court on the grounds that this racial imbalance was actually unconstitutional. They stressed that state death penalty laws violate the Fourteenth Amendment to the Constitution, which guarantees equal protection under the law.

To prove the validity of their point of view, they presented the research conducted by University of Iowa law professor David Baldus. Baldus has studied nearly 2,500 homicides that occurred in Georgia between 1973 and 1979. He found that individuals who murdered whites were eleven times more likely to be sentenced to death than those who killed members of minority groups.

To ensure the accuracy of his findings, Baldus did additional checks on his research data. Documents that included trial transcripts, prison files, parole-board records, as well as other data, were carefully scrutinized. Initial statistical data was reanalyzed in an attempt to rule out any extenuating circumstances that might have influenced the sentencing process—such as giving the death penalty to an individual with a lengthy record or to someone who had committed a particularly brutal murder.

Even taking these factors into consideration, the law professor still found that people who killed whites were at least four times as likely to get the death penalty as the murderers of African Americans.[6] It was also found that African Americans who killed whites were the most likely inmates to be executed. For example, prosecutors sought the death penalty in 70 percent of the cases in which the defendants were African American and the victims were white, but only asked for the death penalty in 19 percent of the cases when a white had been convicted of killing an African American.

Relying heavily on Baldus's findings, these lawyers went before the Supreme Court in 1987 to present the case of *McClesky* v. *Kemp*. Warren McClesky was an African American who had shot a white police officer during a furniture store robbery in Atlanta, Georgia. After McClesky had been convicted and sentenced to death, his lawyers tried to appeal their client's sentence at the federal court level. They presented Baldus's research as the basis of their appeal, but lost. One federal court felt the study was flawed. Another federal court ruled that even if the study was accurate, it was unable to rule out other explanations for why the defendant had received the death penalty.

But at the Supreme Court level, McClesky's defense attorneys stressed that the statistics on the racial imbalance in death penalty sentencing should be sufficient for a finding of bias in their client's case. As one of McClesky's lawyers stated, "Evidence that would amply suffice if the stakes were a job, a promotion, or the selection of a jury should not be disregarded when the stakes are life and death."[7]

While the case was heard, there was good deal of speculation about its outcome. Some in the legal profession felt that too much emphasis had been placed on studies that couldn't possibly account for the individual circumstances affecting each case. As an assistant Georgia attorney general had remarked, "There are simply too many unique factors relevant to each individual case to allow statistics to be an effective tool in proving intentional discrimination."[8]

Yet the opposing viewpoint was perhaps best expressed by George Kendall, an Atlanta attorney for the American Civil Liberties Union, when he stated "One hundred years ago, a White who killed a Black got leniency, but a Black who killed a White got death. There are still strong remnants of that bias."[9]

Various reasons have been cited for racial prejudice continuing to surface in courtroom scenarios. Some individuals feel that public opinion and the manner in which some cases are handled by the media may be pertinent factors. According to a sociologist from the University of Florida, "Prosecutors are political animals. They are influenced by community outrage which is subtly influenced by race."[10] Jurors may be influenced by subtle forms of racism as well. As Welsh White of the University of Pittsburgh Law School stated, "It is built into the system that those in the predominant race will be more concerned about crime victims of their own race."[11]

It may be interesting to note that some white, as well as African American, death row inmates feel discriminated against by the tendency to give more severe sentences to those whose victims were white. In another case heard by the Supreme Court, James Hitchcock, a white on Florida's death row, contended that he'd been victimized by racial bias. Hitchcock was sentenced to death for murdering a thirteen-year-old white girl. He believes that he would have received a lesser sentence if the girl he killed had been African American.

The Supreme Court's reaction to Warren McClesky's appeal was intriguing. The justices did not find fault with the statistical data introduced. They accepted as truth that those who kill whites are eleven times more likely to be executed than those who kill African Americans.[12] Yet the Supreme Court refused to overturn McClesky's death sentence. They ruled that even though discrimination in this area legitimately existed, there was no concrete evidence that any such prejudice had played a role in the McClesky trial.

The Court, which had not been unanimous in the ruling, upheld McClesky's death sentence by a five to four vote. As dissenting Supreme Court Justice William Brennan said of the decision, "It is tempting to pretend that minorities on death row share a fate in no way connected to our own, that our treatment of them sounds no echoes beyond the chambers in which they die. Such an illusion is ultimately corrosive, for the reverberations of injustice are not so easily confined." [13]

His feelings were underscored by numerous individuals within the religious community, who were appalled by the Supreme Court's ruling. As Monsignor Daniel F. Hoye, general secretary of the United States Catholic Conference, stated:

> The fact that capital punishment is applied in a racially discriminatory way has been one of the reasons for our continued opposition on moral grounds to the application of the death penalty. . . . The system under which criminals are sentenced is such that race often plays a prominent role in determining whether they will live or die. . . . we believe that capital punishment under these conditions is surely 'cruel and unusual punishment.' [14]

Nevertheless, for their client's sentence to be overturned McClesky's attorney would have had to prove that either the prosecutor, judge, or jury had been specifically biased against

McClesky because of his race. Statistics and demonstrated patterns of behavior alone had been insufficient to save him.

The case was over, but some important moral questions remained unresolved. Many individuals felt it was blatantly unfair to hold a defense attorney responsible for proving overt racial discrimination on the part of those involved in the judicial process. They'd be faced with a nearly impossible task. As the director of the Southern Coalition on Jails and Prisons described the predicament: "Jurors are going to have to jump up and admit they are racists." [15] Even if such evidence could be amassed in some instances, as death row inmates are frequently poor and minority group members, these individuals are often among those least likely to be able to afford the necessary additional hours of legal expense.

Many in the legal profession were upset by the possible ramifications of the Supreme Court's decision in the McClesky case. For instance, prior to the McClesky decision, some Florida attorneys had raised a related issue. They wondered if all minority group members awaiting execution on death row might be entitled to an automatic review of their case on the basis of racial discrimination.

They had based their argument on a study of sentencing procedures throughout eight states. The pattern of discrimination revealed was similar to the findings of Professor Baldus. According to law Professor Samuel R. Gross of Stanford University, "The discrimination we found is based on the race of the victim, and it is a remarkably stable and consistent phenomenon." [16]

It was hoped that if McClesky's death sentence were overturned, an important precedent would be set regarding this issue. However, that turned out not to be the case. Attorneys charged with proving that those involved in determining their client's sentence had been racially biased now faced a somewhat insurmountable task.

Perhaps one of the best known cases of executed juveniles in which the insinuation of racial bias was especially strong was that of an African American named George Junius Stinney, Jr. As a boy, Stinney had lived with his parents and four brothers and sisters in South Carolina. Although his parents had been sharecroppers, his father also held down a second job working at a local lumber mill. The Stinneys, who were active members of their local Baptist church, had been known as hard-working, religious people.

Yet in March 1949, the family found itself in serious trouble. It all started on the day two young white girls riding a bicycle stopped to ask George, the eldest Stinney boy, where they could find some pretty wildflowers to pick. Supposedly, George led the girls to a heavily wooded area, where he raped and killed them. When the girls' bodies were found in a water-filled ditch the following day, the police picked up George for questioning. While in police custody, he was harshly treated and, after an intensive forty-minute interrogation, had signed a confession.

But in spite of their son's signature on the paper, the Stinney family refused to believe that the confession was valid. They felt their son might have been forced to confess because he feared severe reprisals from his interrogators. George's father later suggested that the two girls might have been murdered by whites, who dropped the youngsters' bodies off in an African American neighborhood to shift suspicion from themselves.

Nevertheless, word of George's confession angered local whites. There was talk of lynching, and some felt that the youth's entire family might fall victim to vigilante justice. In fact, soon after George's arrest, his family was forced to leave the area.

Following Stinney's indictment for the crime, preparations for his trial began. His family was too poor to afford an attorney, so the court appointed a lawyer to represent George. This was an unfortunate turn of events for him. His attorney was a young counselor with minimal courtroom experience.

Having political aspirations of his own, the young lawyer was not happy with his assignment to represent such an unpopular defendant. He would have rather not been associated with the case, but he had little choice in the matter. As a consequence of his attorney's attitude, George Stinney, Jr., ultimately received a poorly prepared defense.

The incident had occurred in March, and the next regularly scheduled court sessions was in late June. But due to the public outcry and the urgent nature of the situation, a special, earlier court session was slated to hear the case. As a result, Stinney's trial began exactly one month after the crime. Twelve white men were chosen to serve on the jury. The prosecution completed its presentation of the case in under half an hour, and Stinney's defense took even less time.

Stinney's lawyer neglected to present any evidence or witnesses to speak on his client's behalf. It's estimated that the jury took a full ten minutes to reach a verdict. Not surprisingly, Stinney was found guilty and sentenced to die.

That was the last time Stinney ever saw his attorney. His legal counsel had never informed his client or any of George's relatives that there were still alternatives open to the young teenager. As a result, no further legal attempts were launched to save the fourteen-year-old's life. Up until the time of his execution, George Stinney, Jr., remained completely ignorant of his right to appeal or challenge his sentence.

While waiting on death row to be executed, George wrote to his mother claiming his innocence. He begged her to do whatever she could to help him. But the family felt helpless against the odds they faced. So they only waited and prayed for their imprisoned son.

However, the Stinney case had received quite a bit of publicity. Some people felt it was morally wrong for our legal system to require a fourteen-year-old to forfeit his life for a crime he might not have comprehended the gravity of. Various organizations, including the National Association for the Advancement of Colored People

(NAACP), sent over fifty letters to the state's governor requesting clemency for the teenager.

Attempting to retain the support of all his constituents, Governor Johnson decided to visit the fourteen-year-old in jail. He claimed that he wished to become more familiar with the circumstances surrounding the case. After reviewing the situation, the governor decided against commuting the sentence. He had determined that the seriousness of the crime overrode much factors as Stinney's youth and inexperience in worldly matters.

But some individuals felt the governor might have weighed other factors in his decision as well. Since he was about to launch a race for the Senate in the next few months, it was strongly suspected that he was somewhat reluctant to make a decision that might result in some unfavorable publicity.

As his execution date drew closer, George Stinney, Jr., confessed his guilt to the crime on a number of occasions. He also spent quite a bit of time studying the Bible and trying to repent for what he'd done. On the day before his electrocution, he told his jailer that he was truly sorry for his actions and that now he only hoped that God, his parents, and the girls' families would forgive him.

At 7:00 A.M. on June 16, 1944, the fourteen-year-old took his last walk. He was led to the death chamber by his jailers. Stinney was carrying a Bible and seemed calmly resigned to his fate.

But everything didn't go as smoothly as planned. A problem developed that had surfaced previously in past electrocutions of juveniles. The chair, which had been designed to kill adults, was too large for a child. And this time prison officials had neglected to have the necessary adjustments made for a youth's electrocution.

George Junius Stinney, Jr., only stood five feet one inch tall and weighed about ninety-five pounds. Therefore, as the prison guards attempted to retain him in the large chair, his small body kept slipping from their hands. As a newspaper reporter described the turn of events,

"He is calm, a relief to the guards, who fumble with the straps designed for larger victims. As the current surges through his body, Stinney's wide-eyed face emerges from under the loosing fitting mask on his head. Tears are flowing from his eyes." [17]

Following his death, George's body was retrieved by his family for a private funeral. Although years have passed since Stinney's execution, some of his family members are still troubled by what happened to their eldest son. They feel that the young teen was railroaded into a quick death and stress the fact that, at fourteen years of age, George was the youngest person ever to be executed in America in this century. As one of his relatives angrily recounted George's demise, "They sat in judgment and killed . . . like they was God. They took him, tried him, and they fried him." [18]

Another capital punishment case with strong racial overtones occurred prior to that of George Stinney, Jr. It involved two Hispanic brothers—Manuel and Fernando Hernandez. Seventeen-year-old Manuel and his eighteen-year-old brother Fernando lived with their mother in a rural part of Arizona. The brothers often hunted together, and one day while out shooting game in a nearby forest, they came across an old prospector sitting at his campfire.

The two quickly devised a plan to rob him. While Manuel tried to distract the man, Fernando came up from behind and struck the prospector over the head. Once he was unconscious they took his money and possessions. Unfortunately, before leaving, Manuel shot the older man, and the brothers disposed of his body in an abandoned well.

Although Manuel had tossed his gun into the bush, police found it the following day, when the prospector's body was discovered. The weapon was traced to Manuel, and he and his brother were arrested and held without bail. As the brothers had been born in Mexico and hadn't been in the United States very long, their English was extremely limited. Therefore, they hadn't had a clear understanding of their present legal predicament, and unfortunately during the early phase of their case, neither was provided with access to an interpreter or legal counsel.

When later represented by court-appointed attorneys at separate trials, both were found guilty and sentenced to die. It's likely that racial discrimination was a factor in why the Hernandez brothers were initially denied their rights and dealt with harshly by the court.

Prior to their execution date, Manuel claimed full responsibility for the crime and swore that his brother hadn't been involved in the killing. But at that point, nothing he said or did could help Fernando. On July 6, 1934, both teenagers were strapped into adjoining chairs in an Arizona gas chamber. The brothers held hands as the poisonous vapor seeped into the small area and died within moments of each other.

Sadly, racism within the criminal justice system can often be largely attitudinal. It compounds the inherent problem as it may be especially difficult to change the bias of a juror, judge, or prosecutor if in some cases he isn't even aware of his prejudice. Some feel it's impossible to devise effective legal safeguards to erase racism from the capital punishment framework. They want the death penalty abolished on the grounds that racist death sentences are unconstitutional.

Many find executions of minority group youths especially offensive as they feel that these young people have often spent their entire lives in disadvantaged environments. As former Supreme Court Justice Marshall stated, " . . . [if most Americans knew] of the disproportionate infliction of the death penalty on the poor, the ignorant, and the underprivileged, they would suffer a shock to their conscience and sense of justice." [19] We are left with the question of whether a society that strives to be humane and democratic can ever afford to allow the color of someone's skin to even indirectly influence whether he or she will live or die.

7

Death Row's Untold Stories

When young people's crimes have been particularly brutal, those in favor of capital punishment for juveniles have stressed the appropriateness of this punishment for youths. In such instances, it may be especially difficult to perceive these individuals as deserving leniency from the criminal justice system. But many young people guilty of capital crimes have an ongoing history of horrendous treatment that has continued throughout their childhood years. Some people feel it's unrealistic to expect a youth who has only known pain and has never been exposed to the benefits of a normal family life to develop and behave normally.

Perhaps one such example is that of Edward Haight, who was executed on July 8, 1943, in New York after being convicted of the kidnapping and murder of two young girls. Haight's family life had been difficult ever since he'd been a toddler. Haight's father had been in and out of prison during most of the boy's childhood. An uncle, who had been close to the immediate family, had also spent ten years in a penitentiary.

When Haight was thirteen, his home burnt to the ground in a fire. Unfortunately, the boy's mother died during the incident. Edward Haight's life, as well as the lives of his brothers and sisters, was taken over by the state. But the Department of Social Services failed to provide him with even a marginally better existence than what he'd already experienced.

Edward, along with his siblings, was shifted through a series of foster home placements. Yet rather than securing the love and stability he desperately needed, frequently the young teen met with severe punishments and abuse in these settings. To make matters worse, by then Edward Haight had already been psychiatrically diagnosed as in the early stages of psychosis. The doctors had also concluded that the youth was incapable of developing sound moral values.

Signs of his disturbed mental state and home life were readily reflected in Edward's disruptive behavior at school. He often acted inappropriately and frequently became involved in violent incidents. It was even rumored that the thirteen-year-old boy had once filled a fountain pen with his own blood. At fourteen, Haight was reexamined by several psychiatrists, who recommended that he be kept under close observation for several years. But, although it was blatantly warranted, Haight was never afforded any type of ongoing psychiatric attention.

Later at his murder trial, Edward Haight's attorney made the following plea to the jury, "I do not ask you to turn this unfortunate boy out. I ask you to return a verdict of not guilty by reason of insanity, so that he can be placed in an institution where he belongs." [1] Instead, the jury found Edward Haight guilty in just under an hour and a half.

The teenager was executed at Sing Sing prison about eight months later. By then, all his appeals, in addition to a request for clemency to the state's governor, had been denied. Edward Haight felt as alone and alienated at the time of his death as he had during his brief life. It was reported that the seventeen-year-old's last wish prior to this execution was to have someone visit him.

It's not uncommon for violent youths to exhibit negative behavioral symptoms in their early years of life. However, in spite of plainly apparent clues throughout a person's childhood, often serious problems remain undetected. In such instances, young people who have already experienced difficulty meeting societal standards are pushed even farther away.

Psychologists have cited that the ability to trust and form normal interactive relationships develops during the first two years of life. At that point, young people have also learned to emphasize or feel for others. By two, children from well-functioning households begin to learn the difference between right and wrong. Frequently, they already realize that their actions have consequences.

Unfortunately, not all children grow up in nurturing environments. Households plagued by such problems as drug and alcohol abuse, economic difficulties, wife and child abuse, or a host of other potentially traumatic situations may not provide an atmosphere condusive to a young person's growth and development. As a result, some children do not develop the ability to feel for others. They may also fail to form important curbs on their behavior.

A vicious cycle of abuse, neglect, and general indifference can leave children emotionally crippled. They may grow into young adults who are filled with rage. One such young person with an early history of aberrant behavior described his home life in this way:

> My father used to beat my mom all the time. That makes me kind
> of angry. He was always out partying, getting high. My fantasy
> is of making him suffer. First, I'd shoot him in the kneecaps and
> let him suffer for about an hour. Then I'd shoot him [again] and
> let him suffer some more, and then I'd put a bullet through his
> head.[2]

The anger they feel may frequently be directed at others outside the home. In a three-year study of 146 young people from physically abusive home environments, it was found that 83 percent of the teenage boys engaged in assaultive behavior toward their girlfriends.[3] Often, they demonstrated a tendency to minimize their abusive actions, while placing the blame for their inappropriate behavior on their victims. One boy justified pulling his girlfriend's hair and tightly twisting her arm by saying, "She made me so mad because she was late for the dance that I thought she shouldn't do that to me again." Another young teen who suspected that his girlfriend had lied to him threw her down a flight of stairs at their junior high school.

Other research on violent behavior has been done by Elise Lake at the University of Washington. Lake conducted a study to learn under what conditions children growing up in violent home environments will later commit violent acts as adults. After questioning 237 prison inmates convicted for violent offenses about their exposure to violence at a young age, Lake concluded that while spanking alone was not necessarily a contributing factor in demonstrated adult violent behavior, intense and severe punishments that entailed punching, kicking, or striking with an object can be. Of the study participant inmates, 87 percent had been subjected to such extreme violence prior to the age of twelve.[4]

An interesting finding of Lake's research was that at times violent adults hadn't necessarily been the direct targets of early childhood violence. Some inmates had witnessed instances of extreme violence between their parents.

In analyzing the survey's results, Lake concluded that violent childhoods sometimes produce violent adults because children tend to model their own behavior after that of the adult role models around them as well as learn what are acceptable reactions from them. The strength of a child's bonds to his parent(s) is still another factor in how effectively a young person will learn to curb his actions. As Lake commented, "If there's a lot of violence in the family, even if it's only observed, it will have a detrimental effect on the child's attachment to the family, which in turn, makes violent or deviant behavior more likely."

Unfortunately, at times innocent victims have become targets for the overwhelming rage of these abused young people. As one psychologist explained the phenomenon, "These children are dead inside. For them to feel alive and important, they engage in terrible types of sadistic activity." [5]

A troubled childhood is perhaps the one thing that most violent youths share. For example, in the case of Ted Bundy, a serial killer executed in Florida, his family firmly insisted that Ted had enjoyed a completely normal childhood and had never shown the slightest sign of deviant behavior. However, near to his execution date, it was revealed that by the time Bundy had turned three years old, he had already been secretly placing knives in his aunt's bed.

In some instances, young people who've been abandoned physically or emotionally by their immediate family may turn to their peers for friendship and acceptance, as well as confirmation of their antisocial values. But often the group's influence has been shown to be especially treacherous. These teens may wind up trying to prove themselves as best they can—and as a result frequently engage in violent behavior.

For example, fifteen-year-old Paula Cooper, the youngest female on death row in decades, was accompanied by three other teenage girls when she robbed and murdered a seventy-eight-year-old Bible teacher in Gary, Indiana. The cruel and senseless killing of the deeply religious elderly woman is impossible to justify. Yet Paula Cooper's lawyer attempted to explain the young girl's actions as he painted a sinister picture of what her own home life had been like.

When Paula and her sister were small, Paula's father beat both girls at whim. Some days he'd use his fists; other times he'd employ an extension cord in this grisly task. The girls' father also repeatedly beat their mother and once even raped the woman in the presence of her children.

Paula's mother felt continually intimidated by her husband. In an effort to end her suffering along with that of her children, one afternoon she took both her daughters out to the garage with her, where she tried to commit suicide in the car through carbon monoxide poisoning. By the time she'd changed her mind, Paula and her sister were already unconscious.

Later on, when the girls repeatedly ran away from home, they were always apprehended by juvenile authorities and returned to their parents. Despite the fact that some school personnel had become aware of the fact that Paula was beaten routinely, there was never a thorough official investigation to determine if she was a victim of child abuse.

As a result, Paula was forced to grow up very much on her own. The teenager's parents were not even present in the courtroom when their fifteen-year-old daughter was convicted of murder and sentenced to die. The attorney handling Paula's appeals feels that the severe child abuse his client endured provides sufficient mitigating circumstances to have the teenager's death sentence overturned. He believes that evidence of her abuse had not been presented strongly enough at the sentencing hearing. As the lawyer stated, "The real crime of this case is that the juvenile justice system allowed this abuse to go on. They [Paula and her sister] complained about the abuse, but nothing ever happened." [6]

Pope John Paul II has attempted to intervene on Paula Cooper's behalf. As the chief spokesperson for the Vatican indicated, "I can affirm that the Holy See and the Holy Father have, through confidential channels, put forward their views, aimed at obtaining clemency for Paula Cooper, underlying the human and humanitarian aspects of the case." [7] The Pope has been supported in his efforts by demonstrators who picketed the American Embassy in Rome on

Paula's behalf. They carried placards that read, "Let Paula Cooper Live" and "Justice Not Revenge."

It may be interesting to note that in Europe the Cooper case has served as a pivotal point in an international protest against the death penalty for juveniles in the United States. Pockets of the pro-Paula movement have sprung up in Spain, Germany, and France, as well as throughout various parts of Italy. More than two million Europeans have signed petitions urging that the youth's sentence be commuted. Numerous reporters from large Italian newspapers have flown to Indiana to interview both Paula and her attorney in order to best present the issues involved.

Many of Cooper's European supporters firmly believe that the girl is a victim of the society in which she was raised. One activist expressed objections about her sentence by saying, "Paula Cooper's color of skin, [she is African American] the fact that she was a minor, and her difficult childhood are all factors in why she shouldn't die." [8]

When she was sentenced, Paula Cooper apologized to her victim's family and pleaded with the judge for mercy. She said, "I didn't go there to take somebody's life. It happened. It just happened. Something—it wasn't planned. We didn't sit up and say we was going to go and kill this innocent old lady. Everybody put the blame on me." [9] But the judge remained unconvinced that Cooper's past could possibly excuse her actions. He said, "We would not want our children to be beaten with extension cords, but we would not expect them to go out and kill little old ladies because of it." [10]

Yet there have been several studies that indicate that youths with troubled pasts and neurological problems frequently end up on death row. One research project involving patients at New York University's Manhattan Psychiatric Center revealed four key risk factors present in an individual's background that might make him or her an especially vulnerable candidate for involvement in violent crime. These were a history of violent suicide attempts, a measurable neurological abnormality, a "deviant" family environment that included such factors as both physical and emotional child abuse, and a young person's exposure to a parent's continued substance abuse.[11]

This study confirmed the results of a survey of juveniles awaiting execution on death row. It was conclusively found that in actuality many of these individuals have hidden histories. According to Dorothy Otnow Lewis of the New York University School of Medicine, "These young [people] . . . often have a history of brain damage, psychiatric disorders, and physical and sexual abuse that has either been unrecognized or deliberately concealed."[12]

Lewis's study demonstrated that many of the youths had suffered head injuries as children. At times, their injuries resulted in hospitalization, indention of the skull, and loss of consciousness. In addition, neurological abnormalities, including evidence of brain injury, abnormal head circumference, and seizure disorders were also documented.

In all young people studied, severe psychiatric disorders were evidenced. Some were psychotic, some had histories of recurrent depression or manic depression, and others experienced bouts of paranoia during which they'd assault imaginary enemies. Many of the juveniles on death row were victims of brutal physical abuse or had been sexually assaulted by older male relatives.

At times, juvenile death row inmates were hesitant to tell the truth about themselves because they wished to avoid the stigma of being categorized as "crazy" or "retarded." In a number of instances, the young people were so ashamed of the way they'd been treated by their families that they had tried to keep their home life a secret.

Lewis, who addressed an annual meeting of the American Academy of Child and Adolescent Psychiatry in Washington, D.C., stated that "the litany of handicaps would undermine arguments for the death sentence."[13] However, in many of these cases, pretrial psychiatric or psychological exams were never performed, and Lewis noted that the evaluations that were done tended to be inadequate.

Perhaps among Lewis's most disturbing findings were the unholy alliances sometimes formed between the families of juvenile death row inmates and prosecutors. Many parents interested in concealing their own poor treatment of their offspring offered prosecutors their full cooperation and even encouraged judges to give their child the death penalty. In return, Lewis described how "on several occasions, attorneys requested that we conceal or minimize parental physical and sexual abuse to spare the family any embarrassment." [14]

Yet, despite these findings, many individuals who favor the death penalty for juveniles do not feel that a difficult home situation and perhaps a neurological disorder give anyone an excuse to commit a brutal murder. Perhaps Indiana Prosecutor Jack Crawford best expressed this viewpoint when he stated, "The hard fact for many in our society to realize is that there are young people who are advanced beyond their years; to the extent that they are capable of conceiving, planning, and carrying out some of the worst crimes imaginable." [15]

Individuals who advocate the death penalty for teenagers guilty of heinous murders stress that a just society cannot afford to forget the victims of unconscionable cruelty. They argue that there were no mitigating circumstances for the victims of these often barbaric teen murders.

However, opponents of the death penalty for juveniles view the situation differently. Their stance on the issue was articulated by Paula Cooper's attorney when he said, "If we as a society really care about the victims of a crime, we will do our utmost to see that children are not raised in the same way Paula Cooper was raised. . . . This is the best way to help victims—to insure that there are no victims." [16]

8

Around the World
and at Home

Like the United States, many countries around the world have grappled with the question of capital punishment and its appropriateness for juveniles. In 1976, our northern neighbor, Canada, abolished the death penalty within its borders. This was a departure from its former policy, which was somewhat similar to that of the United States. Although there's no available statistical data to indicate exactly how many individuals have been executed throughout Canada's history, it's been estimated that between 1867 and 1962 about 450 people were hanged there. Eleven of these individuals were females.

Early on, Canadian public hangings often had the aura of a spectator sport. At the time, Canadian lawmakers believed that the sight of a criminal struggling for life as he dangled from the gallows would serve as a crime deterrent for others. Frequently, the crowd's reaction was reminiscent of that of early executions in the United

States. For example, in 1828, Toronto's population was approximately two thousand. Yet over ten thousand visitors once eagerly journeyed to the city to witness a double execution held there.

Often these spirited spectators arrived at the gallows hours prior to the scheduled event in order to secure a spot with an unobstructed view of the attractions to follow. Although the crowd was usually eager to get a good look at the condemned man, in many instances it was the executioner who stole the show. If the crowd concluded that it had been an efficient, tidy hanging, there were cheers, applause, and whistles for the hangman. Comparably, a sloppy job might draw jeers and boos from the spectators.

In the early 1800s, Canadian justice might have been thought of as somewhat harsh. There were 120 offenses for which an individual might be hanged, and many of these infractions seemed quite innocuous. For example, a person could be executed for defacing a street sign. As in the United States, young people were not spared from the hangman's noose. In 1803, a thirteen-year-old boy was hanged in Montreal following his conviction for stealing a cow.

But with the passage of time, Canadian laws began to reflect the changing values and ideals of the country. Although capital punishment continued, by 1869 public executions had ceased. The last state executions took place in 1962, when two men were hanged in Toronto, and by 1967 capital punishment was banned with the exception of cases in which police or prison guards were murdered. Canadian lawmakers completely abolished the death penalty in 1976.

Yet in recent years, there's been some debate in Canada as to whether capital punishment should be restored. At times, numerous polls have indicated that a solid portion of the population would like to bring back the death penalty. Many Canadians feel that their criminal justice system hasn't adequately upheld the law.

Perhaps indicative of this popular sentiment are the feelings expressed by a retired Canadian farmer whose wife had been run down and killed by an intoxicated driver nearly twenty years ago. Since the police neglected to follow up on the case properly, the drunk driver was never criminally charged. The widowed farmer firmly believes that restoring capital punishment would help assure victimized law-abiding citizens that "the law was in their favor." He feels that presently criminals don't fear the state's retribution, adding that they too often walk into prison feeling, "I'll just put in my time and go out and be twice as bad." [1]

But others, such as Edward Greenspan, one of Canada's most successful criminal lawyers, are adamantly against bringing back the death penalty to their country. He has frequently stressed that Canada's homicide rate has not risen since the abolition of capital punishment in 1976. Although Greenspan realizes that the death penalty has recently been used more frequently in the United States, he strongly warns against this option for Canada. As Greenspan stated, "It's one thing to import clothes and television programs from the United States, but I don't think we have to import their death penalty." [2]

On the other side of the Atlantic, England had an extensive history of invoking the death penalty for a number of offenses until the nation banned capital punishment in 1965. Prior to its abolition, there had been a good deal of debate regarding the country's need to retain as severe a penalty. While both pro and con capital punishment sentiment could be discerned among the English people, several important cases involving the death penalty's application are thought to have influenced public opinion on the issue.

One such instance was that of John Evans, a mildly retarded truck driver who told police that he'd been plagued by a troubled conscience since he murdered his wife. At first, the police and the court found it difficult to believe Evans as he had reported several contradictory accounts of the homicide. One version even implicated his neighbor John Reginald Christe—an upstanding local resident who had served on the police force for a number of years. Yet once the court heard

Christe's claims of innocence and was reminded of his record as a dedicated public servant, he was dismissed as a suspect. As a result, Evans was found guilty, sentenced to die, and later executed.

But the story wasn't over. After a time, several corpses were discovered both in Christe's yard and inside his home. It was soon learned that the man believed to have been an exemplary citizen was actually a ruthless mass murderer. Before long, it was realized that, in all likelihood, Christe had killed Evans's wife while an innocent man was executed for the crime.

Many Britons, dismayed by this apparent travesty of justice, began to question seriously the criminal justice system's ability to ensure fair and equitable trials for all citizens. Shortly thereafter, the public was also given cause to wonder whether innocent individuals had again been executed in two other cases.

After these incidents, arguments to abolish the death penalty seemed to be received more favorably as public opinion shifted in that direction. Then in 1965, England's Parliament voted to ban capital punishment. Yet apparently the action was taken somewhat tentatively as the legislation passed stipulated that the new measure would remain in effect for just five years prior to being reevaluated.

The effects of the ban were inconclusive. During the first few years, the murder rate, as well as that of other violent crimes, soared. Then the trend leveled off, and in the last two years of the five-year trial period, crime in England actually declined. In any case, when the law was reviewed after half a decade had passed, capital punishment remained abolished.

More recently, a movement to reinstate the death penalty has rekindled in England. Some feel this may partly be a response to Irish terrorist acts in English stores, homes, and restaurants. As former Prime Minister Margaret Thatcher said of these deeds, ". . . vicious young people who go out and murder people . . . should not go out in the knowledge that their own lives cannot be forfeited." But at this time no official action has been taken in that direction.

In Germany, capital punishment has been prohibited since the end of World War II, when the new Federal Republic of Germany emerged. As Hitler's regime had been responsible for the slaughter of millions, Germans became conscious of showing the world they were capable of appreciating the sanctity of life. The continued abolition of the death penalty in Germany has evolved as a human rights issue. Attempts to reinstate it have not gathered significant momentum.

Israel also banned capital punishment except in cases involving convicted Nazi war criminals. Under these circumstances, the death penalty's use has been justified on the basis of the atrocities committed against Jews by these individuals during World War II. Although the continuing Arab-Israeli conflict has prompted some discussion of making capital punishment a consequence for Arab terrorist acts, no change has taken place.

However, shifts in national policy on capital punishment have frequently occurred in other countries of the world. Although the majority of nations have done away with the death penalty, some such as the Soviet Union reinstated it following its abolition. Still other nations, such as Spain, have had somewhat of a roller coaster relationship with capital punishment. There the death penalty was abolished in 1932, but just two years later, in 1934, it was reinstated for a number of offenses. In 1938, Spain fully resumed the practice of capital punishment, only to abolish it for a second time in 1978.

Japan has retained the death penalty over a long period of time. There a person may be executed for murder and other crimes that eventually result in a loss of human life. But perhaps due to Japan's lower crime rate, capital punishment is used far less frequently than in America. Usually only a few people are executed annually throughout the nation. Although at times there's been some talk of abolishing capital punishment, this sentiment has not been widespread.

Perhaps the death penalty is most firmly rooted in some Muslim nations, where it's often been a consequence of various infractions of Islamic law. In Iran, under the Ayatollah Khomeini's rule, large numbers of individuals were both tortured and executed for political acts and crimes against the religion of Islam. In an Islamic nation, religion and law are indivisibly intertwined. Therefore, offenses such as adultery (engaging in sexual relations outside of marriage) and disregarding religious principles are seen as extremely grave crimes.

Recently the United Nations altered its stand on capital punishment to reflect a more liberal viewpoint. In the past, the United Nations' position on the death penalty attempted to incorporate the sentiments of countries that wanted capital punishment completely abolished and those that felt it should exist as a penalty for especially heinous crimes, as well as the view of some nations that each country should freely determine its own policy on the issue. Yet the organization still urged that certain safeguards regarding the death penalty be instituted. These were reflected in Article 6 of the UN's International Covenant on Civil and Political Rights (December 6, 1966): "Anyone sentenced to death shall have the right to seek pardon or commutation of the sentence. Amnesty, pardon, or commutation of the sentence of death may be granted in all cases." The UN document also addressed the question of the death penalty for juveniles. It further states: "Sentence of death shall not be imposed for crimes committed by persons below eighteen years of age and shall not be carried out on pregnant women."

Later on, the UN strengthened its official stand to advocate the international abolition of the death penalty. A 1980 *Report to the Secretary General on Capital Punishment* states: "The United Nations had gradually shifted from a position of a neutral observer concerned about but not committed on the question of the death penalty to a position of favoring the eventual abolition of the death penalty."

The policy of executing young people under eighteen years of age has already been widely banned throughout much of the world. Amnesty International, a human rights organization, revealed that from 1978 to 1988 only eight out of 11,000 individuals executed internationally were juveniles. Three of those eight young people were executed in the United States.[3] Other nations that executed juveniles within that time period were Pakistan, Rwanda, and Bangladesh.

It may seem ironic that at a time when most western nations are abandoning the death penalty, the rate of both adult and juvenile executions in the United States is at its highest since capital punishment was reinstated in 1976. The significant increase in the death penalty's popularity may mirror America's response to an increasingly violent society. As one elected official described the trend, "The U.S. doesn't lead the world in education, trade, and health care, but we lead in murders. We are the killing fields of the world."[4]

There also appears to be a general loss of faith in the social institutions relied on in the past to maintain a sense of order within society. Today many people wonder if the present criminal justice system is adequately prepared to keep violent criminals off the streets. Especially in urban areas, where Americans may feel particularly unsafe, increased demands for capital punishment legislation enables them to at least symbolically fight back.

The growing public outcry has prompted an emotionally soothing response from politicians. As one political consultant described it "Both parties have opted for the easy way out—give voters what they want in terms of instant gratifications, including instant death."[5] Even politicians with strong liberal backgrounds may now be found to favor the death penalty. As one governor described the trend that appears to be sweeping the country:

> It's the ultimate political cop-out. It reflects an unwillingness of candidates to propose programs that might actually impact on crime, because that might mean spending money, and that might

mean tax increases. It is easier to hold out a quick fix, the idea
that we will all be well if we just burn people.[6]

Yet some individuals opposed to capital punishment for youths stress that since violent crime is frequently an outgrowth of problematic family relationships and community conditions, the responsibility for improving the situation should be shared. They underscored the need for funding for and the development of innovative programs on the federal, state, and local government level. These programs would have to be reinforced by the efforts of parents, schools, police, churches, business owners, and local civic groups. The challenge is to prevent young people from losing their sense of community and instead help them to develop a stake in both their neighborhoods and their futures. They believe that alienated teens need to be reclaimed as potential assets.

One effective National Crime Prevention Council program known as "Youth As Resources" involves hundreds of teens in Boston and three Indiana cities in activities designed to control crime as well as to improve their living environments. These teens have built a community playground and garden, delivered donated food, and tutored younger children. In other projects, teens produce and perform skits for children on such topics as drug abuse and staying in school. Youths also help the elderly with chores and errands and build inner-city housing for low-income families. Teens with a stake in their environments and futures not only have no reason to resort to violence, but they also have important reasons to avoid it.

While there's obviously not a single simple solution for America's crime problem, opponents of capital punishment for minors believe that such constructive approaches make far more sense than telling youths that we kill people who kill people to show that killing people is wrong. They warn to continue to do so comes at too great cost to our humanity and stature as a nation.

Notes by Chapter

Chapter 1

1. Patricia Scharber Lefevre, "Professor Grapples With Execution of Juveniles," *National Catholic Reporter* (August 1, 1986), p. 4.

2–3. Jack El-Hai, "An Execution of Justice; Once Upon a Time, Minnesota Was a Hangman's State," *MPLS-St. Paul Magazine* (September 1986), p. 104.

4. "Death Row: Last Skirmish, Lawyers Go to the Supreme Court With What May Be the Final Broad Test of Capital Punishment," *Newsweek* (October 20, 1986), p. 34.

5–6. David Gelman, "The Bundy Carnival, A Thirst for Revenge Provokes a Raucous Send-off," *Newsweek* (February 6, 1989), p. 66.

7. Joe Klein, "Hard Time: Getting Tough on Crime," *New York Magazine* (May 8, 1989), p. 18.

8. Daniel N. Van Ness, "Punishable by Death: Constitutional Questions about the Death Penalty May Be Largely Resolved, But the Moral Issues Persist," *Christianity Today* (July 10, 1987), p. 26.

Chapter 2

1–2. Alice Coddington and Lesley Parott, "The Death Penalty: Should Canada Bring It Back?" *Chatelaine* (November 1987), p. 45.

3. Richard Stengel, "Young Crime, Old Punishment," *Time* (January 20, 1986), p. 22.

4. "Kids Who Kill," *Woman's Day* (May 30, 1989), p. 91.

5. Panel on Research on Deterrent and Incapacitative Effects, *Deterrence and Incapacitation; Estimating the Effects of Criminal Sanctions on Crime Rates* (Washington, D.C.: National Academy of Science, 1978), p. 84.

6. John and Kathleen Colligan, "The Death Penalty: Views of a Victim's Parents," *National Catholic Reporter* (December 27, 1985), p. 7.

7. Patricia Lefevere, "Death Penalty Said to Be More Costly Than Life: State Budgets May Impede Executions," *National Catholic Reporter* (February 27, 1987), p. 4.

8. Susan Hansen, "Governor's Beliefs Stop Executions: Anaya's Act Of Mercy Wins Praise and Criticism," *National Catholic Reporter* (December 12, 1986), p. 1.

9–14. United States Code, Title 49 Appendix, 1151 to 1650, 1990.

15–17. Alain L. Sanders, "Bad News for Death Row, The Court Okays the Execution of Teenage and Retarded Criminals," *Time* (July 10, 1989), p. 48.

Chapter 3

1. Charles Whitaker, "Should Teenagers Be Executed?" *Ebony* (March 1988), p. 118.

2. *Clarion* [Mississippi] *Ledger* (January 5, 1947), p. 1.

3. *Elko* [Nevada] *Daily Press* (August 24, 1942), editorial.

4. Laurence Gonzales, "The Executioners; Capital Punishment in Illinois," *Chicago* (March 1988), p. 91.

5. Isabel Wilkerson, "Death Sentence at Sixteen Rekindles Debate on Justice for Juveniles," *The New York Times* (November 2, 1986), p. 26.

Chapter 4

1. Stanford Law Review (November 1987), p. 33.

2. Washington University Law Quarterly, 1985, Vol. 62, p. 21.

3. Donald D. Hook and Lothar Kahn, *Death in the Balance: The Debate Over Capital Punishment* (Lexington, Mass.: Lexington Books, 1989), p. 95.

4. James Baker, "A Movie for the Defense," *Newsweek* (March 13, 1989), p. 27.

Chapter 5

1–2. Richard Stengel, "Young Crime, Old Punishment," *Time* (January 20, 1986), p. 22.

3. Dee Reid, "Low IQ Is a Capital Crime," *The Progressive* (April 1988), p. 25.

4. George Washington Law Review, Vol. 1414 (1985), p. 23.

5–6. Dee Reid. "Low IQ Is a Capital Crime," p. 25.

7. Joe Popper, "Countdown to Death in a Gas Chamber," *National Catholic Reporter* (July 1, 1988), p. 6.

8. *Connecticut Gazette and Universal Intelligencer* (October 20, 1786), p.2.

9. Robert F. Drinan, "Execute an Eight-Year-Old? The John Penry Case," *The Christian Century* (February 22, 1989), p. 199.

10. United States Code, Title 19 Appendix, 1151 to 1650, 1990.

11–12. Dee Reid, "Low IQ Is a Capital Crime," p. 27.

Chapter 6

1. "Race, Death & Justice," *The Progressive,* (June 1987), p. 8.

2. Daniel Van Ness, "Constitutional Questions About the Death Penalty May Be Largely Resolved, But the Moral Issues Persist," *Christianity Today* (July 10, 1987), p. 25.

3. Victor L. Streib, *Death Penalty for Juveniles* (Bloomington, Ind.: Indiana University Press, 1987), p. 60.

4. Clifford Sloan, "Death Row Clerk," *The New Republic* (February 16, 1987), p. 18.

5. Robert F. Drinan, "Racism; One More Reason Death Penalty Must Go," *National Catholic Reporter* (May 22, 1987), p. 12.

6. Richard Lacayo, "Clearing a Path to the Chair," *Time* (May 4, 1987), p. 80.

7–8. "Death Row: Lost Skirmish, Lawyers Go to the Supreme Court With What May Be the Final Broad Test of Capital Punishment," *Newsweek* (October 22, 1986), p. 34.

9–11. Ted Gest, "Black and White Issue? The Supreme Court Wrestles With the Death Penalty and Race," *U.S. News & World Report* (October 20, 1986), p. 24.

12. Daniel Van Ness, "Constitutional Questions About the Death Penalty May Be Largely Resolved, but the Moral Issues Persist," p. 25.

13. Richard Lacayo, "Clearing a Path to the Chair," p. 80.

14. "Thinking About the Death Penalty," *America* (May 16, 1987), p. 393.

15. Richard Lacayo, "Clearing a Path to the Chair," p. 80.

16. "Death Row: Last Skirmish, Lawyers Go to the Supreme Court With What May Be the Final Broad Test of Capital Punishment," p. 34.

17–18. *Sunday Record* [Bergen/Passaic/Hudson Counties N.J.], (March 28, 1982), p. E1.

19. Donald D. Hook and Lothar Kahn, *Death in the Balance: The Debate Over Capital Punishment* (Lexington, Mass: Lexington Books, 1989), p.70.

Chapter 7

1. *North Westchester Times* (November 2, 1942), p. 1.

2. Anastasia Toufexis, "Our Violent Kids," *Time* (June 12, 1989), p. 54

3. Maria Roy, *Children in the Crossfire: Violence in the Home—How Does It Affect Our Children?* (Deerfield Beach, Fla.: Health Communications Inc., 1988), p. 99.

4. "Violence Begets Violence," *USA Today* (December 1989), p. 54.

5. Anastasia Toufexis, "Our Violent Kids," p. 54.

6. Charles Whitaker, "Should Teenagers Be Executed?" *Ebony* (March 1988), p. 122.

7. Roberto Suro, "Pope Urges Indiana Not to Execute Woman," *The New York Times* (September 27, 1987), p. L13.

8. George Hackett, "Indiana Killer, Italian Martyr; A Death Row Cause," *Newsweek* (September 21, 1987), p. 37.

9–10. Isabel Wilkerson, "Death Sentence at 16 Rekindles Debate on Justice for Juveniles," *The New York Times* (November 27, 1986), p. 26.

11. D.D.Edwards, "Advances Reported in Predicting Violence," *Science News* (May 23, 1987), p. 324.

12–14. "Hidden Histories on Death Row," *Science News* (October 31, 1987), p. 287.

15. Charles Whitaker, "Should Teenagers Be Executed?" p. 122.

16. Michael J. Farrell, "Between the Dark and the Daylight on Death Row," *National Catholic Reporter* (March 4, 1988), p. 28.

Chapter 8

1. Mark Nicols, "Should the State Kill?" *Maclean's* (June 29, 1987), p. 16

2. Mary Janigan, "The Death Vote; Capital Punishment—Canadian Parliament Debate," *Maclean's* (March 16, 1987), p. 10.

3. Charles Whitaker, "Should Teenagers Be Executed?" *Ebony* (March 1988), p. 122.

4–5. Steven V. Roberts and Ted Gest, "A Growing Outcry: Give Them Death," *U.S. News & World Report* (March 26, 1990), p. 24.

6. Michael Kramer, "Cuomo, the Last Holdout," *Time* (April 2, 1990), p. 2.

Further Reading

Books

Barden, Renardo. *Gangs.* New York: Crestwood House, 1989.

Bedau, Hugo A., ed. *The Death Penalty in America.* 3rd ed. New York: Oxford University Press, 1982.

Berger, Gilda. *Violence and the Family.* New York: Franklin Watts, 1990.

Hood, Roger. *The Death Penalty: A World-Wide Perspective.* New York: Oxford University Press, 1989.

Kronenwetter, Michael. *Taking a Stand Against Human Rights Abuse.* New York: Franklin Watts, 1990.

Landau, Elaine. *Teenage Violence.* Englewood Cliffs, N.J.: Julian Messner, 1990.

McKissack, Patricia and Fredrick. *Taking a Stand Against Racism and Racial Discrimination.* New York: Franklin Watts, 1990.

Zimring, Franklin, and Gordon Hawkins. *Capital Punishment & the American Agenda.* New York: Cambridge University Press, 1987.

Articles

Barrett, Cindy. "When Death Was a Spectator Sport." *Maclean's*(March 16, 1987), p. 18.

Cohen, Richard M. "Politicians, Voters, and Voltage." *Time* (February 13, 1989), p. 96.

Finn, Peter. "Cruel and Unusual Punishment?" *Scholastic Update* (November 4, 1988), p. 13.

Johnson, Robert. "This Man Has Expired: Witness to an Execution." *Commonwealth* (January 13, 1989), pp. 9–15.

Lefevere, Patricia. "Major Justice Questions Lurk in Some Executions." *National Catholic Reporter* (July 1, 1988), pp. 7–8, ff.

"Murder Most Foul." *The Progressive* (May 1989), p. 10.

Press, Aric. "Execution At an Early Age: Should Young Killers Face the Death Penalty?" *Newsweek* (January 13, 1986), p. 74.

"The Slow Pace of Death Row: A System No One Likes." *Newsweek* (February 8, 1988), p. 64.

Stengel, Richard. "Young Crime, Old Punishment." *Time* (January 20, 1986), pp. 22–23.

"Thinking About the Death Penalty." *America* (May 16, 1987), p. 393.

Van Ness, Daniel W. "Is the Death Penalty Constitutional?" *Christianity Today* (July 10, 1987), p.26.

"Will Drug Dealers Fear the Noose?" *U.S. News & World Report* (October 31, 1988), p.11.

For More Information

Organizations Concerned With Various Aspects of the Criminal Justice System

American Justice Institute
705 Merchant Street
Sacramento, CA 95814
(916) 442-0707

Amnesty International of the U.S.A.
322 Eighth Avenue
New York, NY 10001
(212) 807-8400

Capital Punishment Project
132 W. 43rd Street
New York, NY 10036
(212) 944-9800

Center for Studies in Criminal Justice
University of Chicago Law School
1111 E. 60th Street
Chicago, IL 60637
(312) 702-4444

Death Row Support Project
P.O. Box 600
Liberty Mills, IN 46946
(219) 982-7480

National Center for Juvenile Justice
701 Forbes Avenue
Pittsburgh, PA 15219
(412) 227-6950

National Council on Crime and Delinquency
77 Maiden Lane (4th floor)
San Francisco, CA 94108
(415) 896-6223

National Criminal Justice Association
444 N. Capitol Street, NW, Suite 608
Washington, DC 20001
(202) 347-4900

Index